Jane Austen´s

EMMA

Jane Austen's

EMMA

Adapted for the stage by

Paula K. Parker

WordCrafts Theatrical Press

JANE AUSTEN'S EMMA

SPECIAL NOTE

Anyone receiving permission to produce **Jane Austen's Emma** is required to give credit to the Author as the sole and exclusive Author of the Play on the title page of all programs distributed in connection with performances of the Play and in all instances in which the title of the Play appears for purposes of advertising, publicizing or otherwise exploiting the Play. The name of the Author must appear on a separate line, in which no other name appears, immediately beneath the title and in size of type equal to 50% of the size of the largest, most prominent letter used for the title of the Play. No person, firm or entity may receive credit larger or more prominent than that accorded the Author.

Jane Austen's Emma

Cover art - "Reflections On Beauty" by Auguste Toulmouche
Public Domain

Published by WordCrafts Theatrical Press
912 E. Lincoln St.
Tullahoma, TN 37388
www.wordcrafts.net

Characters
(in order of appearance)

Mr. Woodhouse
Emma Woodhouse
Mrs. Bates
Miss Bates
Mr. Knightley
Mr. Elton
Harriet Smith
Mrs. Goddard
Mr. Weston
Mrs. Weston
***Isabella Woodhouse Knightley**
***John Knightley**
Jane Fairfax
Frank Churchill
Mrs. Elton
***Mr. Cole**
***Mrs. Cole**

***Note:** *The Knightleys and the Coles make brief appearances; it is suggested to double-cast these four roles.*

ACT I
Scene 1

Setting: A parlor at Hartfield, home of Mr. Woodhouse and his daughter Emma. Mrs. Bates and Miss Bates are guests. Everyone is drinking tea and do not see Mr. Knightley enter until he speaks.

Mr. Knightley:
What I want to know is, who cried the most at the wedding?

Ad Lib:
Knightley! Mr. Knightley! When did you return! How was your trip?

(Mr. Knightley bows to the ladies and nods to Mr. Woodhouse, greeting each by name.)

Emma:
How did you find my sister and your brother?

Mr. Knightley:
Isabella is recovering from giving birth to your namesake quite nicely, Emma. John is a proud father, as he was with the other four. They send their best love to you both and look forward to seeing you once Isabella and the baby can travel.

Emma:
I look forward to seeing all of my nieces and nephews, as well as Isabella and John.

Miss Bates:
Ah, a new baby! We are all looking forward to seeing little Miss Emma Knightley. I'm certain she is a beauty. In fact, Mother and

I were talking about her just yesterday and Mother said, "I'm certain that, if she is named for Miss Woodhouse, then she is certainly a beautiful baby."

(turns to Mrs. Bates)

Didn't you say that little Miss Emma Knightley was as beautiful as her aunt?

Mrs. Bates:

(turns towards her daughter, confused from not hearing properly)

Pork!

Miss Bates:

(slightly embarrassed)

Mr. Perry encouraged Mother to include more pork jelly in her diet.

Mr. Woodhouse:

Mrs. Bates, has the right of it; listen to Mr. Perry. Who would know better about what is good for one's health than the apothecary? Not that everyone listens. I warned poor Miss Taylor not to serve cake at her wedding, for Mr. Perry states that cake would disagree with one's digestion; but she would not listen and insisted on a wedding cake.

Emma:

Miss Bates, allow me to refill yours and your mother's tea. Father, what would a wedding be without a cake?

Mr. Knightley:

Which brings me back to my original query about the wedding. How was it?

Miss Bates:

It was a beautiful wedding. The church altar was decorated with lovely white roses. And Miss Taylor's gown…

Mr. Woodhouse:
(interrupts)

Ah! Poor Miss Taylor. Tis a sad business.

Mr. Knightley:
Poor Mr. and Miss Woodhouse, I know you will miss her, but I cannot agree with 'poor Miss Taylor.' I have a great regard for both of you, but I'm sure Miss Taylor is happy to have only one person to please and not two.

Emma:
(laughs)

Especially when one of those two is a fanciful, troublesome creature, which is *exactly* what Mr. Knightley would call me were Mrs. Bates and Miss Bates and my father not nearby. Mr. Knightley loves to find fault with me.

Miss Bates:
Surely not…

Mr. Knightley:
Emma, I have known you since you were born and as one who is nearly a brother to you, I must behave as a good brother and point out your faults, when I see them. But to get back to the more pleasant topic, I am sorry I missed the wedding. I am certain every friend of Miss Taylor must be glad to have her so happily married.

Emma:
And one matter of considerable joy for me is that I made the match.

Mr. Knightley:
Made the match?! You made a lucky guess.

Emma:
A lucky guess is never merely luck. There is always some talent in it. Have you never been pleased when you made a lucky guess,

Mr. Knightley? When so many people said that Mr. Weston would never marry again, I knew he would. I am quite pleased.

Mr. Woodhouse:
I still cannot understand why Miss Taylor would wish to be married and leave us and her home here at Hartfield? She has been with us since your mother – God rest her soul – passed when you were an infant.

Emma:
Father, I am one and twenty; I no longer need a governess. I daresay that Mrs. Weston wishes to have children of her own.

Miss Bates:
Ah, children!

Mr. Woodhouse:
Why would she want children, when they are always bringing disease into whatever room they enter? Pray do not make any more matches, my dear. They are silly things and break up one's family circle grievously.

(Emma crosses to refill her tea; Mr. Knightley follows. Mr. Woodhouse talks to Miss and Mrs. Bates.)

Mr. Knightley:
Emma…from the expression on your face, I wager that you are not going to gratify your father's request. You're going to continue making matches.

Emma:
I will only make matches for those who need my help. I know! What about Mr. Elton the vicar? He has been in Highbury for a year and has fitted his house so comfortably that it would be a shame to have him single any longer. When he was performing the wedding ceremony this morning, I noted that he looked as if he would like to have the same pleasure for himself.

Mr. Knightley:
Emma, invite Mr. Elton to dinner; that will be a kindness enough.

Mr. Woodhouse:

Mr. Knightley, did I tell you what Mr. Perry said about the benefits of a bowl of warm gruel?

Mr. Knightley:
(to Emma)

Take my advice, Emma. Invite Mr. Elton to supper. Help him to decide between the fish and chicken, but leave him to choose his own wife. Depend upon it, a man of seven and twenty can take care of himself.

(turns and crosses to Mr. Woodhouse)

Now sir, what did Mr. Perry say?

Emma:
(sipping tea and smiling to herself)

Oh I'll invite Mr. Elton to supper. But whether seven and twenty or seven and seventy, in my experience - with the exception of yourself, Mr. Knightley - I have yet to meet a man who is able to adequately care for himself.

Scene 2

(A parlor in Hartfield, a week later. Emma and Mr. Woodhouse are hosting an evening of cards and supper. Mr. Woodhouse, Mrs. Goddard, Harriet Smith, Mr. Weston, Mrs. Weston and Mr. Knightley are present. Emma is greeting guests. Mr. Elton enters.)

Emma:
Mr. Elton, how nice to see you.

Mr. Elton:
Ah, Miss Woodhouse. It was so kind of you and your father to invite me.

Emma:
You are too kind, Mr. Elton. It is merely an evening of cards and a light supper.

Mr. Elton:
As a single man, it is a privilege to exchange a vacant evening for the elegancies and society of your drawing room.

Emma:
My father and I are always happy for your company. Mr. Elton, there is someone whom I wish you to meet. (crosses with him to Harriet) Miss Smith, this is our vicar, Mr. Elton. Mr. Elton, this is Miss Harriet Smith. (bows/curtsy) Harriet is a former pupil at Mrs. Goddard's school and has stayed on as a boarder. I am convinced that she and I are to become fast friends. Mr. Elton, Miss Smith has expressed an interest in arranging flowers for the church's altars. Mrs. Goddard tells me her ability is unsurpassed.

Harriet:
Your praise is too kind, although I do enjoy arranging flowers.

Mr. Elton:
If Mrs. Goddard and Miss Woodhouse recommend you, then I'm certain you are superb.

Emma:
If you will excuse me, I must see about setting the tables for cards.

Mr. Elton:
I would be most happy to assist…

Emma:

No indeed; deciding the flowers for the altar is quite important.

(Mr. Knightley is wandering by)

Mr. Knightley will be happy to help me.

(Emma and Mr. Knightley cross to the card tables and begin placing cards and counters on each table.)

Mr. Knightley:
(half voice)

Emma…what are you doing?

Emma:
Doing? Why, merely introducing Harriet into Highbury society. Our community is so small and everyone knows everyone. I am looking forward to getting to know her better.

Mr. Knightley:
And there is no match making involved?

Emma:
I don't know what you are talking about, especially since you have already stated that I have no skills as a match maker. If I introduce two people and they form an attachment to each other, what am I to do?

(Mr. Knightley opens his mouth and Emma interrupts)

I must gather everyone for cards; Father will be most concerned if supper is served late. Would you please finish dividing the counters for the tables?

(Emma leaves before he can say anything and calls the guests to the tables. Mr. and Mrs. Weston. Harriet and Mr. Elton are at one table. Mrs. Goddard, Emma, Mr. Knightley and Mr. Woodhouse are at the other. After ad libbing beginning to play cards, conversation resumes.)

Mrs. Weston:
Ah Emma. I've been meaning to tell you our news. We had a letter from Mr. Churchill.

Emma:
How is your son?

Harriet:
Your son? I understood you recently married.

Mr. Weston:
You see, Miss Smith, my first wife – God rest her soul – passed shortly after the birth of our only son Frank. I had an estate to manage and knew nothing about raising an infant. The Churchills – who are my late wife's brother and his wife and had no children of their own, offered to take the whole care of little Frank. The Churchills have taken good care of Frank and he has wanted for nothing.

Harriet:
What a kind thing for the Churchills to do, although I am certain you miss your son.

Mr. Weston:
Indeed I do. I have seen him time to time. However, since the passing of his uncle, Frank has not been able to visit as much. He has been a great support to his aunt. Indeed, her need for him was so great that he could not attend our wedding.

Mrs. Weston:
But he wrote the kindest letter, congratulating us and stating that he looked forward to meeting his new mama.

Emma:
Everyone in Highbury longs to meet Mr. Churchill.

Mr. Weston:
Then you will be happy to know that we heard from Frank this morning; he is indeed coming to visit us.

Ad Lib:
Ah how wonderful. I can't wait to meet him.

Mrs. Goddard:
It sounds as if Highbury is to be doubly blessed with visitors, for this morning Miss Bates told me that they had a letter from Miss Jane Fairfax. She is coming to visit them soon as well.

Mr. Elton:
Ah, I've heard of Miss Fairfax.

(turns to Harriet).

Mrs. Bates is the widow of the former vicar of Highbury and as such, I feel it is my responsibility to visit them weekly.

Mrs. Goddard:
We all love Mrs. Bates and Miss Bates. I will introduce you to them soon, my dear.

Mr. Elton:
Miss Jane Fairfax is the orphaned daughter of Jane Bates Fairfax and Lieutenant Fairfax. Mrs. Bates is her maternal grandmother and Miss Bates is her aunt.

Harriet:
She does not live with her grandmother and aunt?

Mrs. Goddard:
No, she does not. Miss Bates and her mother had not the means to support Miss Fairfax after the death of her parents. However, Colonel Campbell, who had been a friend of her father, offer to provide for the whole of Jane's education. She has been living with the Colonel and Mrs. Campbell and their daughter and visits her grandmother and aunt from time to time. But she is faithful to write them each week.

Emma:

(with subtle sarcasm)

Which Miss Bates is so kind as to read to anyone within listening distance.

Mr. Knightley:

(understands the sarcasm; speaks in half voice)

Emma….

Emma:

(feigned innocence)

I only speak the truth. And unless one has to be somewhere else soon, they will have the *good fortune* to hear Miss Fairfax's letter more than once within the hour.

Harriet:

To be able to write one's own letter! I love getting letters, but I am not very good at writing them. When I visited the Martins last summer, I was fortunate to have Miss Martin help me compose letters to Mrs. Goddard and tell her of the wonderful time I was having.

Emma:

The Martins? I do not believe I have met them.

Mr. Woodhouse:

Here! Are we going to discuss letters or are we going to play cards? If we wait much longer, supper will be served too late. Mr. Perry always said that a late supper is not good for one's digestion.

(ad lib discussion about the cards, laying down cards, etc.)

Emma:

Miss Smith, you must come to see me soon. I vow we will discover much we have in common.

Mr. Knightley:

(in half voice)

I'm sure you will.

Scene 3

(The flower garden at Hartfield, several weeks later. Harriet is posing in Grecian costume, holding a vase, while Emma paints her portrait.)

Harriet:
I have enjoyed my visits to Hartfield these past few weeks, Miss Woodhouse. Your welcome has made me feel most at home.

Emma:
I am happy to hear that, Harriet. When Miss Taylor married Mr. Weston, I did not merely lose a governess. I lost a dear friend and daily companion. While I love my father's company, he does not care to discuss gowns and hairstyles and…other topics dear to a woman's heart.

Harriet:
I am happy to discuss whatever topic you wish.

Emma:
Tell me about yourself. You say you do not know your parents?

Harriet:
No… Mrs. Goddard said I must not ask. But they provide well for me, so I fancy they are a good family.

Emma:
Indeed they must be.

(pause)

Since we cannot talk about your family, tell me of your other acquaintances. You spoke of the Martins?

Harriet:
They are the kindest of people. They provide Mrs. Goddard's school with eggs and cheese from their very own farm.

Emma:

They are farmers?

Harriet:

Indeed and with such a delightful house. Mrs. Martin has *two* parlors, one of them quite as large as Mrs. Goddard's drawing room. They have eight cows – Mr. Martin was so kind as to show me around the farm - and one a very pretty little Welsh cow. They have a summer house, with roses growing around the sides that Mr. Martin planted, where we all drank tea.

Emma:

How kind of Mr. Martin to plant roses for his wife.

Harriet:

(confused for a moment)

Oh, no; Mrs. Martin is not his *wife;* she is his mother.

Emma:

I…see…And…what kind of man is Mr. Martin?

Harriet:

(clasps the vase to her chest)

Oh, the kindest…

Emma:

Hold still please.

Harriet:

(laughs)

I am sorry.

(moves back into her pose)

Mr. Martin is the kindest of men, so obliging and good-humored. One day, he walked three miles in order to bring me some walnuts because he heard me say how much I liked them. His mother and sisters are very fond of him. Mrs. Martin told me one day that it was impossible for anyone to be a better son and therefore she was sure

(suddenly shy)

that he would make a good husband.

Emma:
High praise indeed, but one would expect a mother to believe that of her son. What sort of looking man is Mr. Martin?

Harriet:
It is strange; at first, I thought him very plain, but now I do not think him plain at all. But have you never seen him? He is in Highbury every now and then and he knows you by sight.

Emma:
My dear Harriet; I may have seen him fifty times, but without having any idea of his name. Farmers are precisely the order of people with whom I feel I can have nothing to do. A degree or two lower and I might be useful to their families in some way or other. But a farmer can need none of my help.

(pause)

While I wish him all the best, I cannot hope one of my friends would consider marrying Mr. Martin, or any farmer, for then I would never be able to see either of them in society.

(Mr. Woodhouse enters)

Mr. Woodhouse:
Ah, there you are my dear. How do you do, Miss Smith?

Harriet:
How do you do, Mr. Woodhouse?

Emma:
Hello, Father. Are you returning from your walk?

Mr. Woodhouse:
Yes, indeed. Mr. Perry declares that three turns around our lawn

each day is sufficient for exercise yet not enough time to breathe in anything harmful.

(notices Harriet's outfit)

But, Miss Smith, where is your shawl?

Emma:
Father, you know Harriet is posing for me. She is a young Greek maiden.

Mr. Woodhouse:
Do Greek maidens not wear shawls? How else do they protect themselves from ill drafts?

Emma:
But it is a warm day, Father, and I am nearly finished.

Harriet:
I am flattered that you would wish to paint my portrait, Miss Woodhouse.

Emma:
I would say, "You're welcome," had the idea originated with me. But you must remember that it was Mr. Elton's suggestion. It was when you and he were here for tea and I was showing you our portrait gallery. I mentioned that I used to paint portraits and thought you would be a lovely subject for a painting. Do you remember what Mr. Elton said?

Harriet:
(blushes)

I do not believe I do.

Emma:
Ah…although I would hate to name it a falsehood, from your blushes, I believe you do remember. He said, "It would be delightful! Let me entreat you, Miss Woodhouse, to exercise so charming a talent in favor of your friend."

Harriet:
It was a kind thing for Mr. Elton to say; and so eloquent. I could never grow tired of listening to him speak.

Emma:
I agree. Most ministers are experienced in speaking in public, but I vow Mr. Elton is superior to all I have heard. When he decides to marry, his *wife* will have the pleasure of listening to him all day long.

Mr. Woodhouse:

Well, you can enjoy listening to him today, for I see Mr. Elton and Mr. Knightley walking across the lawn.

(Mr. Elton and Mr. Knightley enter. Greetings bows/curtsies)

Mr. Woodhouse:
Mr. Knightley, have you come for your daily game of backgammon?

Mr. Knightley:
I could not sleep last night, after you beat me soundly and was determined to come earlier, in order to challenge you to a rematch.

(notices the canvas)

What are you doing, Emma? Painting?

Mr. Elton:
Miss Woodhouse was so kind as to acquiesce to my request to paint Miss Smith's portrait. I have been at Hartfield every day during the painting, longing for the day when the masterpiece would be finished. When I learned it would be completed today, I resolved to be one of the first to see the finished work.

(looks at the painting over Emma's shoulder)

It's perfect!

Mr. Knightley:

(looking at the painting)

You painted her too tall. Come, Mr. Woodhouse, let us get you indoors.

(Mr. Knightley and Mr. Woodhouse start to exit.)

Mr. Elton:

(looks at the painting)

Perhaps Miss Woodhouse wished to use height to allude to Miss Smith's character.

(Mr. Knightley and Mr. Woodhouse exit.)

Emma:

Although I am accustomed to Mr. Knightley's critiques, it is for that very reason I no longer paint portraits. Whenever I painted anyone, there was generally a wife or husband about, finding fault with my work. One reason I agreed to paint Harriet's portrait was that no husbands or wives would be present.

Mr. Elton:

(looks at the back of Emma's head and smiles)

No husbands or wives…yet.

(Emma looks at Harriet and they smile. Harriet lowers her head shyly.)

Emma:

Once the paint has dried, all that will be required is for us to get it to London to have it framed.

Mr. Elton:

Miss Woodhouse, might I be trusted with the commission?

(Emma and Harriet look at each other and smile again.)

Emma:

You are too good, Mr. Elton.

Mr. Elton:

Indeed, it would bring me *infinite* pleasure to be employed with such a task. If we could retire to your portrait gallery where we can discuss the merits of the various frames there? The frame for this masterpiece must be perfect!

(Mr. Elton picks up the canvas and carries it off stage. Harriet crosses to Emma.)

Harriet:

How…*kind* Mr. Elton was in his praise.

Emma:

Kind? My dear Harriet, I am a great observer of people and I can assure you that what Mr. Elton expressed was not kindness.

Harriet:

(open eyes wide)

What do you mean?

Emma:

Unless I am very much mistaken – and I do not believe I am – I think Mr. Elton's *wife* will soon have the pleasure of listening to him speak all day long.

Scene 4

(The flower garden at Hartfield, several weeks later. Emma is carrying a basket of cut flowers when Harriet enters, very excited.)

Emma:

Harriet! You are early. I did not expect you until tea this afternoon.

Harriet:

Pray forgive me, Miss Woodhouse, but something extraordinary has happened and I had to see you immediately.

Emma:
Well, let us at least sit down and allow you to catch your breath.

(They walk to a small bench and sit. Emma places the basket on the ground.)

Now, what has happened?

Harriet:
I went to the tailors this morning, to be fitted for a new gown. When I got back to Mrs. Goddard's I learned that a letter was left for me.

(in a burst of excitement)

He has proposed to me!

Emma:
What? Already? Mr. Elton has not wasted any time…

Harriet:
Oh no; the letter is not from Mr. Elton. It's from Mr. Martin! Who would have thought it? I was so surprised I did not know what to do. It is a very good letter, at least I think so. He wrote as if he really loved me, but I do not know, so I came as fast as I could. Will you read the letter? Pray do so.

(She hands the letter to Emma, who unfolds it and reads.)

Is it a good letter? Or is it too short?

Emma:
(slowly)

Yes, indeed, a very good letter. So good that I think one of his sisters must have helped him; yet it is not the style of a woman. Vigorous, decided, with sentiments to a certain point.

(hands the letter back to Harriet)

A better written letter than I expected.

Harriet:
Well…well…and what shall I do?

Emma:
What shall you do? Do you mean with regard to this letter?

Harriet:
Yes.

Emma:
You must answer it, of course, and speedily.

Harriet:
But what shall I say? Dear Miss Woodhouse, do advise me.

Emma:
Oh no, no. The letter had much better be all your own. Your meaning must have no doubts, and include such expressions of gratitude and concern for the pain you are infliciting.

Harriet:
(looking down, disappointed)

You think I ought to refuse him then?

Emma:
Ought to refuse him! My dear Harriet, what do you mean? I thought – I beg your pardon – perhaps I have been under a mistake. I thought you were consulting me only as to the wording of the letter. You meant to return a favorable answer, then?

Harriet:
No, I do not. That is, I do not mean…What shall I do? Pray, dear Miss Woodhouse, tell me what I ought to do?

Emma:
I shall not give you any advice, Harriet; that is a point which you

must settle with your own feelings.

Harriet:

(slowly, contemplating the letter)

I had no notion that he liked me so very much.

Emma:

I lay it down as a general rule, that if a woman *hesitates* as to whether she should say, "Yes," to a man, then she should say, "No." I thought it my duty as a friend to say thus, but do not imagine I want to influence you.

Harriet:

Oh no! I sure you are a great deal too kind to – but if you would just advise me - no, no, I do not mean that – as you say, one should not be hesitating – it is a very serious thing – it will be safer

(slows down)

…to say

(looks at Emma uncertainly)

"No," perhaps? Do you think I should say, "No?"

Emma:

Not for the world would I advise you. If you prefer Mr. Martin to every other man, if you think him the most agreeable man you have ever been in company with, why should you hesitate? You blush, Harriet. Does anybody else occur to you at this moment? At this moment, whom are you thinking of?

(Harriet looks at her shyly)

I think you know the answer as well as I.

Harriet:

Since you will not give me your opinion, then I must do as well as

I can by myself. I have now quite determined - and have almost made up my mind – to *refuse* Mr. Martin. Do you think I am right?

Emma:
Perfectly right, my dearest Harriet. While you were in suspense, I kept my feelings to myself, but now you are so completely decided, I have no hesitation in approving. Indeed, it would have grieved me to lose your acquaintance, which must have been the consequence of your marrying Mr. Martin.

Harriet:
I never thought of that before. Dear me – how should I have ever borne it! It would have killed me never to come to Hartfield anymore.

Emma:
Thank you, my dear Harriet; we shall not be parted. A woman need not marry a man merely because she is asked or because he can write a tolerable letter.

Harriet:
That is true. I am quite determined to refuse him.

Emma:
There will be no difficulty in the answer and it should be written directly.

Harriet:
But what shall I say? I am not skilled at letter writing.

Emma:
(stands)

Then let us go into the parlor immediately and I will be happy to render what assistance I may.

Harriet:
(stands, a little sad)

Whilst I am determined to refuse him, I do not want to hurt him.

Emma:
Then let us think of those among our absent friends who are more cheerfully employed. At this moment, perhaps, Mr. Elton is showing your portrait to his mother and sisters, telling them how much more beautiful the original is.

Harriet:
Surely not!

(shyly)

Do you think so.

Emma:
Unless I am very much mistaken – and I do not believe I am – that picture is Mr. Elton's companion, his solace, his delight. It introduces you to his family. I feel I can safely assure you that, when Mr. Elton returns, he will not need a *letter* to express his intentions.

Scene 5

(The parlor in Hartfield the next day. Emma is attempting to read when Mr. Knightley enters.)

Emma:
Mr. Knightley!

Mr. Knightley:
Emma. I do hope I'm not interrupting anything important?

Emma:
No indeed. Father is out for his daily walk around the yard and I am reading. Miss Bates is forever proclaiming how well read Miss Fairfax is and I am determined to read more. Mrs. Weston was forever encouraging me to read more.

Mr. Knightley:
Do not allow me to interrupt you. I can walk with your father.

Emma:
No, please, do come and sit down.

(puts a marker in the book and sets it down).

I have read Dr. Johnson for nearly a quarter of an hour; surely that is sufficient reading for one day.

(She crosses to the tea table, pours a cup, and carries it to Mr. Knightley.)

Mr. Knightley:
(trying to be serious)

I am certain Mrs. Weston would be most pleased.

(They both sit)

Mr. Knightley:
Where is Miss Smith today?

Emma:
She was here earlier, but was obliged to go to Mrs. Goddard's for an hour or two. We are going to spend time this evening working on the book that contains her collection of riddles.

Mr. Knightley:
I must say, Emma, your influence over Miss Smith has been quite beneficial. I cannot rate her beauty as you do, but she is a pretty little creature. I am inclined to think well of her disposition. She does you credit; you have cured her of her school-girl's giggle.

Emma:
(slight laugh)

Thank you. I should be mortified indeed if I did not believe I had been of some use.

Mr. Knightley:
You are expecting her again, you say?

Emma:
Any moment now. She has been gone longer already than she intended.

Mr. Knightley:
Something may have happened to delay her; some…visitor, perhaps.

(pause, smiling)

I must tell you that I have good reason to believe your friend will soon hear of something to her advantage.

Emma:
Indeed? Of what sort?

Mr. Knightley:
(still smiling)

A very serious sort, I assure you.

Emma:
Very serious! I can think of but one thing…

(excited)

who makes you their confidant?

Mr. Knightley:
I have reason to think that Harriet Smith will soon have an offer of marriage and from a most unexceptional quarter; Robert Martin. During her visits to the Martin farm, he fell in love with her and means to marry her.

Emma:
He is very obliging, but is he sure that Harriet means to marry him?

Mr. Knightley:
He came to see me at Donwell Abbey two evenings ago. He is one of my tenants and an excellent young man. He told me of his feelings for Miss Smith and asked my advice on marrying her. I had no hesitation in advising him to marry. It is not unlikely that he should be at Mrs. Goddard's today, speaking to Harriet.

Emma:
I will tell you something in return for what you have told me. Mr. Martin spoke to Harriet yesterday – that is, he wrote his proposal in a letter – and was refused.

Mr. Knightley:
What?

(stands, paces across the room)

Then she is a greater simpleton than I ever believed her. What is the foolish girl about?

Emma:
To be sure, it is incomprehensible that a woman should refuse an offer of marriage. A man believes a woman is always ready for anyone who asks her.

Mr. Knightley:
Nonsense! A man does not imagine any such thing! But Harriet Smith refusing Robert Martin is madness. I hope you are mistaken.

Emma:
I saw her answer; nothing could be clearer.

Mr. Knightley:
(stops pacing and stares at Emma)

You *saw* her answer? You *wrote* her answer! Emma, this is your doing. You persuaded her to refuse him.

Emma:

If I did – which I am far from allowing – I should not feel I had done wrong. Mr. Martin is a very respectable young man, but I cannot admit him to be Harriet's equal.

Mr. Knightley:

No, he is not Harriet's equal, for he is her superior in sense and in situation. What are Harriet's claims, either of birth, nature or education? She is the natural daughter of nobody knows whom, with no settled provision and certainly no respectable relations. She is pretty and she is good tempered and that is all.

Emma:

Mr. Martin may be the richest of the two, but he is undoubtedly her inferior as to rank in good society. If she married him, it would be a degradation of the sphere in which she moves.

Mr. Knightley:

A degradation for a woman of illegitimacy and ignorance to be married to respectable, intelligent gentleman-farmer?

Emma:

Although in a legal sense, Harriet may be illegitimate and called Nobody, there can scarcely be a doubt that her father was a gentleman of fortune. That she is a gentleman's daughter - that she associates with gentlemen's daughters - no one will deny that she is superior to Mr. Robert Martin.

Mr. Knightley:

Whoever might be her parents, it does not appear to be any part of their plan to introduce her in what you would call good society. After receiving an indifferent education, she was left in Mrs. Goddard's care to shift as she can. Her family thought this good enough for her. She desired nothing better for herself, until you chose to turn her into a friend. She was happy at the Martin's this past summer; she had no notion of superiority then. Vanity working on a weak mind produces every kind of mischief. You have been no friend to Harriet Smith, Emma.

Emma:

You are unjust. As you describe Harriet – only pretty and good-natured – let me tell you they are not trivial recommendations to the world. I am very mistaken if your sex in general would not think such beauty and such temper the highest claims a woman could possess.

Mr. Knightley:

Men of sense, whatever you may choose to say, do not want silly wives. Better to be without sense than to misapply it as you do. I have kept my thoughts to myself, but I now perceive that it will be fortunate indeed if Harriet receives another offer of marriage.

Emma:

There are those, besides Mr. Martin, who have shown an interest in Harriet.

Mr. Knightley:

Who?

(pause)

Mr. Elton?

(Emma doesn't respond)

Elton is a good sort of man – and a respectable vicar of Highbury – but I am convinced he does not mean to throw himself away on an imprudent match. He has told me often that his sisters are acquainted with a large family of young ladies who all have twenty thousand pounds apiece.

(He picks up his hat and crosses to the door and then turns back to Emma)

This is not your 'guessing' with Miss Taylor and Mr. Weston; I am very much afraid you will find your *matchmaking* ending poorly for all concerned.

(exits)

Scene 6

(The parlor at Highbury. Emma and Harriet are sitting and attempting to read, but appear bored.)

Emma:

(lowers her book)

"All intellectual improvement arises from leisure."

(Looks at the cover of the book.)

I do think Dr. Johnson has the right of it. And I believe we should put his wisdom into practice.

(She places her book on the table and stands.)

Come, Harriet, let us work on your collection of riddles.

(Harriet sets her book down and they cross to the table, where a 'scrapbook' is placed.)

Harriet:

Well, Mrs. Goddard speaks highly of Dr. Johnson.

Emma:

Mr. Elton also speaks highly of him.

(Harriet smiles shyly.)

What an amusing pastime, collecting riddles and placing them within a book.

(They flip a page or two of the book when Mr. Woodhouse enters the room.)

Mr. Woodhouse:
Ah, there you are, Emma, Miss Smith. Staying indoors, I see; good girl. Mr. Perry warns against over exposure to the out of doors.

Emma:
We are working on Harriet's book of riddles, Father.

Mr. Woodhouse:
That is nice.

(He reaches into his pocket and takes out a folded piece of paper.)

I was just coming to find you when this message from Mr. Elton was delivered. It says, "Miss" with a blank line drawn after it. I'm not certain whom it is for.

Emma:

(crosses to her father to get the paper.)

Thank you, Father. You were coming to find me, you say?

Mr. Woodhouse:
Yes. I wanted to ask that you request Cook to make some more thin gruel. Mr. Perry encouraged me to have a bowl each evening before bedtime. He states it induces a sound sleep.

Emma:
I will speak with her.

Mr. Woodhouse:
Well, enjoy yourselves. I will be in my study until teatime.

(He exists. Emma crosses back to the table and sits down.)

Harriet:
Would you like me to give you privacy to read your letter from Mr. Elton?

Emma:
I am certain this is not for me, but for you.

(hands it to Harriet)

Harriet:
Me? But it was delivered here and not to Mrs. Goddard's.

Emma:
Mr. Elton stopped by last night to play a game of backgammon with Father. He asked what you and I were doing to occupy our time, now that your portrait was finished. I told him you were coming here today to spend time reading and working on your collection of riddles. I suggested he might compose a riddle to add to your book and he said he would be most happy to do so.

(gestures to the letter)

Well, are you going to open it?

Harriet:

(looks at it and then thrusts it in Emma's hands)

I cannot. I am all a-tremor. Please, Miss Woodhouse, read it for me.

Emma:

(takes the letter and unfolds it. She scans it for a second and then smiles.)

As I thought, it is a riddle for your book. Listen: *To Miss…*

(pause)

I think we know whose name he wishes placed there. *My first displays the wealth and pomp of kings, Lords of the earth, their luxury and ease.* Well that is clear enough to understand…

Harriet:

(confused)

It is?

Emma:
Yes, for where do kings take their ease?

Harriet:

(thinks for a moment)

At their hunting lodges?

Emma:

No, silly. At their 'court.' Now for the next line, *Another view of man my second brings, Behold him there, the monarch of the seas!*

Harriet:

Monarch of the seas. Can it be Neptune? Or a mermaid? Or a shark?

Emma:

Mermaids and sharks! Nonsense, My dear Harriet, what are you thinking of? He means a 'ship' plain as can be. Now you see, do you not?

Harriet:

Ship? Court? Court? Ship?

(Her eyes widen in understanding. Excited)

Courtship! He means courtship!

Emma:

There can be no other meaning. I am very happy.

(hugs her)

I congratulate you, my dear Harriet, with all my heart.

Harriet:

I suppose, and believe, and hope it must be so. It is so much beyond anything I deserve. Mr. Elton, who might marry anybody. I am sure, a month ago, I had no idea myself.

Emma:

I *had* an idea. In fact, almost from the moment I introduced you to Mr. Elton, I had an idea that something would come of this.

(under breath)

I wonder what Mr. Knightley will say to this?

Harriet:

(confused)

What?

Emma:

(startled, not realizing she was overheard.)

Nothing. I just remembered a recent discussion Mr. Knightley and I had.

(smiles to herself)

Scene 7

(Several months later. Emma and Harriet – dressed in cloaks and warm gloves - are walking across the stage, carrying baskets loaded with food, i.e. breads, vegetables, etc.)

Emma:

Thank you for visiting the poor in town with me, Harriet.

Harriet:

It is sad that at Christmas time so many people are suffering from lack of food and warm clothing. I love Christmas. All the festive decorations and parties and gifts. It is my favorite holiday. And I look forward to meeting your sister and her husband and children. You must be excited about their visit.

Emma:

I am. Ever since Isabella married Mr. Knightley's brother, John, and moved to London, I only see her a few times each year.

Harriet:

But you visit them in London, do you not?

Emma:
No, I have not. In fact, I have never been outside of Highbury.

Harriet:
Truly?

Emma:

Father does not care to leave home and, should I travel anywhere, he would be sick with worry that something untoward happened to me.

Harriet:
When you marry, perhaps you will go somewhere wonderful on your wedding trip.

Emma:
I do not intend to marry.

Harriet:
Do you not? But you are so beautiful and charming.

Emma:
I thank you, but my being charming is not quite enough to induce me to marry. I must see somebody very superior to anyone I have seen to be tempted.

(recalls who she is speaking with)

Mr. Elton, you know, is out of the question.

Harriet:
It is so odd to hear a woman talk so…

Emma:
I have none of the usual inducements of women to marry. Were I to fall in love, indeed it would be a different thing, but I have never been in love. And without love, I am sure I would be a fool to change my situation. Fortune, I do not want; employment I do not want; consequence I do not want. I believe few married women

are half as much mistress over their husband's house as I am of Hartfield. And never could I expect to be so truly beloved as I am by my father.

Harriet:
But then, to be an *old maid* like Miss Bates.

Emma:
This is a formidable image, Harriet and if I thought I should ever be like Miss Bates – so silly, so smiling, so prosing – I would marry tomorrow. But I shall not be a *poor* old maid and it is poverty only which makes celibacy contemptible. A single woman, with a narrow income must be a ridiculous old maid; but a single woman of good fortune, is always respectable.

Harriet:
How shall you employ yourself when you grow old?

Emma:
I do not perceive why I should want more employment at forty or fifty than I have at one and twenty. I shall be very well off, with all of the children of my beloved sister to care for. I shall make certain to always have a niece or nephew about.

Harriet:
Are you acquainted with Miss Bates' niece, Jane Fairfax?

Emma:
We are always *forced* to be acquainted with her whenever she comes to Highbury. Heaven forbid that I should ever bore people with stories about Isabella and her family the way Miss Bates does about Jane Fairfax! One grows sick of the name of Jane Fairfax! Every letter from her is read forty times over. Her compliments to all friends go round and round. Whenever she sends her aunt or her grandmother the simplest of gifts, one hears of nothing else for a month! I wish Jane Fairfax very well, but she tires me to death!

(Mr. Elton enters and walks towards them.)

Emma:
Ah, Harriet, here comes a pleasant change for our thoughts.

(calls to him)

Hello Mr. Elton.

(He crosses to them. Ad lib greetings bows/curtsies)

Mr. Elton:
How delightful on such a dreary morning to come upon a ray of sunshine. But what brings you ladies out on this cold wintry day?

Harriet:
Miss Woodhouse—

Emma:
(interrupts)

—accompanied Harriet on her regular visit to the Graham's cottage. It is hard enough for the family to be poor, but with the wife and mother ill...

(Harriet looks startled.)

Mr. Elton:
An act of Christian charity on the eve of Christmas. How kind of you! May I be permitted to accompany you ladies for a few minutes? You could tell me how you found Mrs. Graham? Mr. Perry told me she was improving somewhat.

Emma:
Oh!

(stops and looks down at her shoes)

I believe the lacing on my boot has snapped. Pray go ahead. I will repair it and follow in half a minute.

(Mr. Elton and Harriet walk on talking quietly.)

Emma:

(to herself)

How fortunate for Mr. Elton to meet us while Harriet was on a charitable mission. It will cast her in a good light as the prospective wife of a minister. I should not wonder if this will bring about an opportunity for a declaration on his part. I will give them a moment longer and then follow behind them slowly.

(After another moment, she walks slowly towards them. Mr. Elton and Harriet have paused and appear to be deep in conversation, he speaking with much enthusiasm and she listening intently. Emma tries to approach unobtrusively, so as not to interrupt.)

Mr. Elton:
…I assure you, it was my dearest wish…

Harriet:
Truly?

Emma:
Can it be? Can he be proposing?

(she steps closer and hears)

Mr. Elton:
…the Cole's were serving beetroots! My favorite!

(Mr. Elton and Harriet laugh and then see Emma)

Harriet:
Were you able to repair your bootlace?

Emma:
I was.

Mr. Elton:
Miss Woodhouse, I made a confession to Miss Smith and now I

must make it to you as well. I told Miss Smith that I was in my parlor, working on my sermon for Sunday, when I looked through the window and saw you two ladies go by. As I had been indoors for the whole morning, I felt a sudden need to get out of doors and determined purposely to follow you.

Emma:
We are happy you did, Mr. Elton.

Mr. Elton:
Now, however, I must leave you. These few minutes with you were a rejuvenation for my spirit and mind and now I feel certain I can finish my sermon by tea.

(tips his hat)

Good day, Miss Smith…Miss Woodhouse.

(Emma and Harriet ad lib curtsies and goodbyes. Mr. Elton exits. Emma and Harriet turn and look at each other, smiling.)

Scene 8

(The parlor at Hartfield. Mr. Woodhouse, Emma, Mr. John Knightley and Isabella Knightley are seated. The ladies have tea, the men glasses of port. Mr. Woodhouse has a bowl of thin gruel.)

Mr. Woodhouse:
Isabella, my dear, what a sad change you have found at Hartfield since you were here last, since poor Miss Taylor has left us. It is a grievous business!

Isabella:
How you must miss her, Father. And Emma too! What a dreadful loss to you both. But I hope she is pretty well.

Mr. Woodhouse:
Pretty well, my dear, but I do not know whether Mr. Weston's home agrees with her.

John:
I do not understand this, 'poor Miss Taylor' business. I thought Randalls a well-kept estate. Are there any concerns as to the air at the Westons' home?

Emma:
Oh no! None in the least. I never saw Mrs. Weston looking better in my life. Father is only speaking his regret.

Isabella:
Do you see Mrs. Weston often?

Mr. Woodhouse:
Not near so often, my dear. Randalls is so far away.

Emma:
Father, Randalls is a mere half mile. And we have missed seeing them but one day since they married.

Mr. Woodhouse:
I cannot deny that poor Miss Taylor does come and see us often; but then, she is always obliged to go away again.

Emma:
Well, you will see her tomorrow night, when we all go to Randalls for the Westons' Christmas Eve supper.

Isabella:
And will Mr. Churchill be present? You wrote that the Westons were expecting him to visit.

Emma:
He has not been here yet.

Mr. Woodhouse:
He writes frequently to his father and poor Miss Taylor. She

showed me the last letter they received. I thought it very well done of him, but whether it was his own idea or his aunt's I do not know. He is but young.

Emma:
Father, Mr. Churchill is three and twenty. You forget how time passes.

Isabella:
Writing his father and new mama is quite pleasing and proper. I am sure it is a comfort to both Mr. and Mrs. Weston. Perhaps he will come while we are here. And Emma, will we meet your new friend, Miss Smith, at Randalls tomorrow night?

Emma:
Alas, no. She was invited, but she sent a note this morning, explaining that she has come down with a cold and Mrs. Goddard insists that she stay in bed.

Mr. Woodhouse:
Indeed she should! A cold is not to be treated lightly; it could develop into a putrid throat. Has Mr. Perry been called to attend her?

Emma:
He has, Father, and was the person to suggest she stay in bed. I am so sorry that you will not be able to meet Harriet, Isabella.

Mr. Woodhouse:
She is such a pretty kind of young person and a wonderful companion for Emma. And when Miss Jane Fairfax arrives – for Miss Bates assures me she is coming to visit soon, now that Colonel Campbell's daughter is married - and then Emma will have her choice of companions.

(Mr. Knightley enters.)

Isabella:
Ah, Mr. Knightley, how are the children? It was so kind of you to

offer to see them to bed.

Mr. Knightley:

Little Emma easily fell asleep in my arms. As to the rest; I am happy to report that, after several stories and one sword fight – which, much to my embarrassment I lost – I was able to convince my nieces and nephews that it was time for them to go to bed. They are wonderful children; John, Isabella, you are quite blessed.

John:

Thank you, George.

Isabella:

How kind of you to say so; but then, one would think you are biased, for you are a fond uncle.

Emma:

Although Mr. Knightley and I disagree on men and women, when it comes to our nieces and nephews, we never disagree.

Mr. Knightley:

(crosses to the side table and pours a glass of port. Emma stands and crosses to refill her tea. They sit away from the others, who are talking among themselves. Emma and Knightley talk to each other.)

If you were as much guided by nature in your estimate of men and women as you are of these children, we might always think alike.

Emma:

To be sure, our discords always arise from my being in the wrong.

Mr. Knightley:

Yes,

(smiling)

and with good reason. I was sixteen years old when you were born.

Emma:

And no doubt you were my superior in judgment at that time but does not the lapse of one and twenty years bring our understandings a good deal nearer?

Mr. Knightley:

I still have the advantage of you by sixteen years' experience.

(smiles to show he is teasing)

The next time I see our youngest niece, I will tell little Emma that she ought to set you a better example than to be renewing old grievances.

Emma:

She will certainly grow up to be a better woman than her aunt. As to the *grievance* of which you speak, as far as good intentions go, we were both right. I only hope that Mr. Martin is not very bitterly disappointed.

Mr. Knightley:

(frowns slightly)

I have never seen a man more disappointed.

Emma:

I am sorry to hear that and hope that he finds happiness soon. Come,

(extends her hand)

let us shake hands and let us make up.

Mr. Knightley:

(takes her hand)

Ah Emma, I cannot stay angry with you.

Emma:

Good, for I would not wish to have you angry with me during

Christmas. Will we see you tomorrow night at the Westons' Christmas Eve supper?

Mr. Knightley:
You will. I have offered Mrs. Bates and Miss Bates to ride in my carriage. I believe it will snow and would not want them to be walking.

Emma:
How kind of you.

(pauses, slightly sarcastic)

Elsewise they would be forced to stay home and *how* could we enjoy Christmas without hearing about Jane Fairfax?

Scene 9

(Randalls – the home of Mr. and Mrs. Weston – decorated for Christmas. Mr. Weston, Mrs. Weston are greeting their guests. Mr. Woodhouse, Mr. John Knightley, Isabella, Emma and Mr. Elton. Ad lib greetings about Christmas, party, etc.)

Mrs. Weston:
Ah my dear Emma; it's so nice to see you. How are you?

Emma:
I am well, Mrs. Weston. But I fear I am the bearer of sad news. Our dear Miss Smith will not be here tonight. She is still in bed with a severe cold.

Mrs. Weston:
How dreadful. I am sorry to hear that.

Emma:
I went to see her earlier and she said Mr. Perry insisted she remain

in bed again today. She asked that I send you her regrets for not attending your lovely party.

Mr. Weston:
She will be missed.

Mrs. Weston:
How kind of you to visit her.

Mr. Elton:
That is what I said when Miss Woodhouse told me the news.

Emma:
I promised to visit her as soon as possible and entertain her with a description of this evening.

Mrs. Weston:
What a good friend you are.

(Mrs. Bates, Miss Bates and Mr. Knightley enter.)

Mr. Weston:
Mr. Knightley! So glad to have you at our little supper.

Mrs. Weston:
And it was so kind of you to bring Mrs. Bates and Miss Bates.

Miss Bates:
Hello Mr. Weston, Mrs. Weston. Yes, indeed, Mr. Knightley was so very kind and thoughtful of our every comfort. He provided a warmed brick wrapped in flannel for Mother's and my feet. Quite warm and toasty

(turns to her mother, raising her voice a bit)

Wasn't Mr. Knightley's carriage warm, Mother?

Mrs. Bates:
(startled)

Pork!

Miss Bates:

(little laugh, pats her mother's arm)

No, Mother. If you recall, we had pork yesterday.

(to Mrs. Weston)

Miss Woodhouse sent over the loveliest pork roast yesterday. It was so kind of her. Mother and I do love pork.

(They all move into the room and begin talking with each other.)

Isabella:
Mr. Weston, Emma and Father tells me that you've heard from Mr. Churchill and are expecting a visit from him soon?

Mr. Weston:
Yes, we are. In fact, we received a letter from Frank just this morning.

Emma:
You did?

(Mr. Elton crosses to Emma during Mr. Weston's following lines)

Mr. Weston:
Yes. Frank wrote to tell us that his aunt was feeling better. You recall that she had been suffering since the death of Mr. Churchill. Well, he said…

(his dialogue continues ad lib during Emma and Mr. Elton's following lines.)

Mr. Elton:
Miss Woodhouse…

Emma:

(turns to him)

Yes, Mr. Elton?

Mr. Elton:
Are you warm?

Emma:
Yes, thank you.

(she turns back to listen to Mr. Weston)

Mr. Weston:
...and then he wrote that he expected to be...

Mr. Elton:
Miss Woodhouse?

Emma:

(turns to him)

Yes, Mr. Elton?

Mr. Elton:
Shall I see whether your father has need of anything?

Emma:
You are so kind, Mr. Elton

(looks towards her father, who is being tended to by Mrs. Weston and Miss Bates),

but I believe between Mrs. Weston and Miss Bates, Father is perfectly content.

(she turns back to Mr. Weston)

Mr. Weston:
...Mrs. Weston was pleased to write back and say...

Mr. Elton:
Miss Woodhouse?

Emma:

(turns to him, trying to contain her frustration)

Yes, Mr. Elton?

Mr. Elton:

Is there anything you need?

Emma:

(pause)

Yes, Mr. Elton. Would you be so kind as to bring me a cup of Mrs. Weston's hot rum punch?

Mr. Elton:

I shall do so immediately.

Emma:

Pray do not hurry, Mr. Elton. I would not wish, in your haste, for you to spill some punch on yourself or on Mrs. Weston's rug.

Mr. Elton:

You are too kind.

(He crosses to the table with the punch. Emma turns back to Mr. Weston.)

Mr. Weston:

Mrs. Weston couldn't be more pleased.

Isabella:

I am sure she could not.

Mrs. Weston:

(stands)

If you would all be so kind as to follow me to the dining room, supper is ready.

(Mr. Weston crosses to Mrs. Weston and leads her off stage, with everyone following, ad lib comments about supper, etc. Mr. Elton rushes to Emma and offers his arm, which she takes reluctantly. Mr. Knightley offers his arm to Miss Bates and Mrs. Bates. When the last person exits, the lights dim for a moment or two and then come back up as they all return to the room, ad libbing about a wonderful meal, etc. Emma is speaking with Mr. Weston.)

Emma:
What a delightful meal. Even Father ate some of the mutton.

Mr. Weston:
Indeed it was. Mrs. Weston was concerned over the whole evening – as new brides are wont to be with their first real supper party – and I told her it would be fine. Indeed, the only thing we needed to make this a perfect evening was your pretty friend, Miss Smith, and my son. I believe you did not hear me telling your sister that we are expecting Frank? We had a letter from him this morning and he will be with us within a fortnight.

Emma:
What a great pleasure it will be to you! And Mrs. Weston is so anxious to become acquainted with him.

Mr. Woodhouse:
Mr. Weston! Do come and hear what Mr. Perry said about asparagus.

(Mr. Weston crosses to him. Mr. Knightley crosses to look out the window. Mrs. Weston and Isabella stay with Emma)

Mrs. Weston:
As I tell Mr. Weston, while I am indeed anxious to meet Mr. Churchill, we are by no means sure of seeing him. It depends upon his aunt's spirits.

Isabella:
Everyone knows of Mrs. Churchill. I pity your son, Mrs. Weston. To be constantly living with a sickly, ill-tempered person must be dreadful. To keep him from visiting his father.

Emma:
He ought to come, even if he could stay only a couple of days.

(Mr. Elton crosses to Emma.)

Mr. Elton:
Miss Woodhouse?

Emma:
Yes, Mr. Elton?

Mr. Elton:
I profess myself to be extremely anxious about your lovely and most amiable friend, Miss Smith. Have you heard anything about her since we have been at Randalls?

Emma:
(relieved to hear him speak of Harriet)

No, Mr. Elton, I have not, which I must take as good news, for I am sure Mrs. Goddard would have sent word if Harriet had grown worse.

Mr. Elton:
I am relieved to hear that.

(turns to Mrs. Weston)

Mrs. Weston, would you please give me your support? Would you please add your persuasions to mine, to induce Miss Woodhouse not to go to Mrs. Goddard's until it was certain that Miss Smith's disorder was not infectious? Miss Woodhouse is so scrupulous for others and yet so careless for herself. Is that fair, Mrs. Weston? Have not I some right to complain?

Mr. Knightley:

(turns back to the room)

It is snowing heavily now, with a strong wind. Mr. Weston, Mrs. Weston, you might have guests for Christmas morning.

(The following lines are spoken almost over each other.)

Mr. Woodhouse:
Stay for the night?

Isabella:
I cannot spend the night away from my children.

Mr. Weston:
I wish the roads were impassable, that you would all stay the night. Don't you agree, my dear Mrs. Weston?

Mr. Woodhouse:
My dear Emma, what is to be done?

Mrs. Weston:
Mr. Weston, as much as I would love the company, we do not have sufficient guest rooms.

John:
We had better order the carriages, my dear. We'll ride in the carriage with your father and see him safely home. Emma…

Mr. Elton:

(interrupts)

I'll be happy to escort Miss Woodhouse home in the second carriage.

John:
Thank you, Mr. Elton.

(Everyone exits with general goodbyes, comments about the lovely evening, safe travels and Merry Christmas)

Scene 10

(The parlor at Hartfield, also with Christmas decorations. The lights are darker, suggesting nighttime, with a single candle burning, to provide light. Two small loveseats are facing each other in front of the fireplace. Emma enters, quite upset. She paces back and forth, removing her cloak and gloves, talking to herself.)

Emma:

What a wretched business, indeed! Such an overthrow of everything I had been wishing for. Such a development of everything most unwelcome! What was Mr. Elton thinking? He must have consumed too many cups of rum punch and Mr. Weston's good wine.

(Emma sits down on the side of one of the loveseats.)

He had barely waited until we were seated in the carriage…

(The lights come up a bit and change to a different color, to suggest a memory. Mr. Elton enters and sits next to Emma, grasping her hand.)

Mr. Elton:

How fortunate to find ourselves in this situation, my dear Miss Woodhouse.

Emma:

(pulls her hand back)

What do you mean, Mr. Elton?

Mr. Elton:

(grasps her hand again)

It must be a sign from above, an answer to all my prayers. For I do not think I could wait any longer. Indeed, I will take advantage of this precious opportunity to declare sentiments which I am sure must already be well known.

Emma:

Mr. Elton, I do not know what you mean. Release my hand!

(she stands and crosses to the other loveseat and sits down.)

Mr. Elton:

Surely you do, my dear Miss Woodhouse…or dare I call you, my dear Emma?

Emma:

No you may not! You do not know what you are doing, Mr. Elton. You drank too much wine.

Mr. Elton:

If I drank too much of anything, it was your beauty.

(He crosses to sit next to her and tries to grab her hand. She tries to keep it out of his reach).

For months I have been hoping, fearing, adoring, ready to die if you refuse me.

Emma:

(gets up and moves to the other loveseat.)

I am very much astonished, Mr. Elton. This to *me?* You forget yourself and mistake me for Miss Smith.

Mr. Elton:

Miss Smith? What do you mean?

(stands and crosses to the other loveseat.)

Emma:

Mr. Elton, this is the most extraordinary conduct. After your behavior this past month to Miss Smith, such attentions to her, such compliments you have spoken to her; to be addressing me in this manner!? Believe me, sir, I am far from gratified in being the object of such professions.

Mr. Elton:

Miss Smith? I never thought of Miss Smith in the whole course of my existence. I never paid her any attentions, but as your friend. Indeed I never cared whether she were dead or alive, but as your friend. If she has fancied otherwise, I am very sorry, but

(he crosses and sits next to her, grasping her hand)

oh, Miss Woodhouse! I have thought only of you. Who can think of Miss Smith when Miss Woodhouse is near. Everything I have said or done for these many weeks past, has been with the sole view of showing my adoration of you.

(Emma pulls her hand back and stands to cross to the other loveseat. When he stands, she holds her hand out.)

Emma:

No! Sit!

(He does. Emma turns away and covers her eyes.)

Emma:

Have I indeed been so blind as to not have seen this?

(Mr. Elton quietly stands and crosses to sit next to her. He waits a moment and then leans towards her)

Mr. Elton:

Charming Miss Woodhouse; allow me to interpret this silence. It confesses that you have long understood me.

Emma:

(lowers her hand)

No sir, it confesses no such thing. Now go over there and sit.

(he does)

Far from having long understood you, I have been in a most complete error till this very moment. Am I to believe that you have never sought to recommend yourself particularly to Miss Smith? That you have never thought seriously of her?

Mr. Elton:

(offended)

Never, madam! I assure you. *I* think seriously of Miss Smith? She is a good sort of girl, but I am not quite so much at a loss as to be addressing myself to Miss Smith. My visits to Hartfield have been for yourself and the encouragement I receive...

Emma:

(interrupts)

Encouragement? Sir, you have been entirely mistaken. I have seen you only as the admirer of my friend. I had no thoughts of matrimony for myself. I pray you will never speak to me of this again.

(They sit silently for a few seconds, looking away from each other.)

Here we are at your house. Good night, Mr. Elton.

Mr. Elton:

(stands)

Good night, Miss Woodhouse.

(He exits. The lights return as they were at the beginning of the scene.)

Emma:

What a wretched business indeed. Such a blow for Harriet! I care not for Mr. Elton's feelings; I am certain he cared only to enrich himself. And will soon try for another lady with ten or twenty thousand. But Harriet! My poor Harriet! Mr. Knightley was right about Mr. Elton and about my interference. Here I have actually talked poor Harriet into believing Mr. Elton in love with her. Harriet might never have thought of him – hoped of marriage with him - but for me. I will *never* play matchmaker again. But poor Harriet; how can I soften the news?

END OF ACT I

ACT II
Scene 1

(The parlor at Hartfield. Emma, Harriet and Mr. Woodhouse are seated, drinking tea.)

Emma:
I am so glad the weather and your health have improved. I missed you dreadfully over the holidays.

Harriet:
I missed you as well, Miss Woodhouse and am sorry that I was unable to meet your sister and her family.

Emma:
They were sorry not to meet you as well, but once the weather cleared, they returned home.

Mr. Woodhouse:
Ah, poor Isabella. How hard it must be for her to leave Hartfield. To pass her life with those she loves, full of their merits, blind to their faults and always innocently busy. She is the model of a perfect wife and mother, just as my late wife was, God rest her soul.

(sighs)

I miss her already.

Emma:
(crosses to tuck a blanket around him)

Father, you can be at peace; I will be here to care for you as good as Isabella. I never see any of your faults and consider you filled with merits.

Mr. Woodhouse:
(slight laugh)

Ah, I'm sure if he were here, Mr. Elton would chide you for falsehoods; I am not perfect.

(He doesn't notice the uncomfortable expression that Emma and Harriet share.)

Speaking of Mr. Elton, I had a letter from him this morning.

(picks up a letter on a side table to read aloud)

He sent his compliments and said that he was proposing to leave Highbury for Bath. "In compliance with the pressing entreaties of some friends, I have engaged to spend a few weeks. I regret the impossibility – due to various circumstances of weather and business – of taking a personal leave of you, sir, of whose friendly civilities I shall ever retain a grateful sense. If you have any commands while I am in Bath, I should be most happy to attend to them."

(folds the letter)

Mr. Elton must have been in quite a hurry to leave that he did not send his compliments to both you young ladies. I pray he has a safe journey, though I do not understand everyone traveling here and there.

(stands)

Ah well, I have had my tea and now it is time for an nap; Mr. Perry tells me that resting after consuming any food or drink is always good for the digestion. Miss Smith, I do hope you will stay for supper?

Harriet:
Thank you, Mr. Woodhouse. I would like that immensely.

Mr. Woodhouse:
Fine. Then I will see you later.

Emma:
Rest well, Father.

(Mr. Woodhouse exits)

Emma:
My dear Harriet, I am so sorry. Father has no idea of what occurred between Mr. Elton and myself; elsewise, he never would have read that letter aloud to you.

Harriet:
That is alright Miss Woodhouse.

Emma:
I can only repeat my abject apologies for the whole mess in making you think Mr. Elton cared for you.

Harriet:
Miss Woodhouse, please. There is no need to apologize again.

(takes a handkerchief and dabs at her eyes)

I blame nobody, certainly not you nor Mr. Elton. Indeed, I do not consider myself as having anything to complain of. To have the affection of such a man as Mr. Elton would have been too great a distinction; I never could have deserved him. It was so kind of you to think otherwise.

Emma:
Harriet, when we first met, I had hoped to teach you, but now I see I have much to learn from you.

Harriet:
You are too kind, Miss Woodhouse.

(pause)

Do you think Mr. Elton is…meeting young ladies? I know I have no right to wish otherwise, but it makes my thoughts low.

Emma:
Then I know just what to do to lift your thoughts.

(stands and pulls Harriet to her feet.)

We shall go and visit Miss Bates and her mother. Miss Bates will talk and talk about Jane and we will be able to think of nothing else.

(They put on cloaks and cross to Miss Bates' house. They knock on the door and Miss Bates answers.)

Miss Bates:
Ah, Miss Woodhouse, Miss Smith!

Emma:
Hello, Miss Bates. After the weather has kept us indoors so many days, we thought to come and visit you and see whether you have a letter from Jane.

Miss Bates:
How kind of you. Do come in.

(She keeps talking as they enter)

Mother and I have not received a letter from Jane; but you should not despair, for we have an ever better replacement.

(Lights come up on interior of Miss Bate's home; Mrs. Bates and Jane Fairfax are sitting. Mrs. Bates is knitting or crocheting in the corner.)

Jane arrived this morning!

(Ad lib greetings/curtsies among the three younger ladies. They sit.)

Emma:
How was your journey, Miss Fairfax?

Jane:
It was—

Miss Bates:

(interrupts)

Jane had a wonderful journey. She had caught a cold, poor thing, did you not, my dear?

Jane:

Well, I did

Miss Bates:

She bore up well, did you not, for you wrote us about it.

(She picks up a stack of letters and rifles through them until she finds the right one.)

Ah, yes, this is the letter we received last Tuesday. You remember Mother? It was last Tuesday.

Mrs. Bates:

(looks up from her knitting/crocheting and yells)

Pork!

Miss Bates:

(laughs)

Oh no, Mother; we didn't have pork that day. We had pork on Monday. Tuesday we had soup; but it was made from pork, so I guess you are right. "Pork" indeed! After luncheon you said I could not have heard from Jane lately because it was not her time to write. And I answered, "But indeed I have; we received a letter this morning." I do not know that I ever saw anybody more surprised. "Have you indeed," you asked and I replied, "Upon my honor!"

(laughs and then unfold the letter to read)

Jane, you wrote that you caught a cold in November and you said you had never been quite the same since.

(to ladies)

How sad to have a lingering cold, do you not agree?

(they open their mouths and she continues reading)

She had not told us about it because she did not wish to alarm us.

(to the ladies)

That is just like Jane; she is so considerate.

(goes back to reading)

However, she was so far from well, that her kind friends, the Campbells, thought she had better come home and see whether the air here would agree with her. They sent her by way of Bath, so she could drink the healthful waters before coming to Highbury.

(folds up the paper)

I would have come to Hartfield to tell you and Mr. Woodhouse our exciting news, but the weather prevented me. And here you are, Miss Woodhouse, Miss Smith, to enjoy our good fortune at having our sweet Jane restored to us.

(She sighs. Everyone waits a moment for her to say something more. When she does not, Emma turns to Jane.)

Emma:
I am so glad you arrived safely. Your aunt and grandmother always tell us of where you go and whom you meet.

Jane:
They are so kind—

Miss Bates:
(interrupts)

Speaking of meeting, Jane, tell them who you saw in Bath.

Jane:
I saw—

Miss Bates:
(interrupts)

Mr. Elton! She saw our own Mr. Elton in Bath. She has been telling us that she saw him often in company and was a great favorite among the young ladies.

(Harriet gasps slightly)

Miss Bates:
Miss Smith are you alright?

Harriet:
Yes…that is, no…that is…

Emma:
She is….hungry…are you not, Harriet?

Miss Bates:
Ah, then she should have a slice of this cake Mrs. Cole brought us this morning.

(She continues talking as she crosses to the tea table and cuts a small slice of cake and takes it to Emma and then returns and cuts one for Harriet.)

Mrs. Cole was just here before you and brought us this lovely cake. She was so good as to sit an hour with us and get reacquainted with Jane and she had a piece of the cake as well. Mrs. Cole, not Jane,

(laughs)

although Jane had a slice too, so I was right on both counts.

(laughs)

Miss Cole was so kind as to say she hoped that Miss Woodhouse and Miss Smith would do us the favor of eating a piece when next they came. And here you are and here's your slice of cake.

Harriet:
Thank you. That was kind of Mrs. Cole to bring you a cake. Mrs. Goddard often praises Mrs. Cole's cakes.

Miss Bates:
Then Mrs. Goddard will be happy to hear that Mrs. Cole told me she plans to bake cakes to serve at the ball. (turns to Jane) How fortunate that you arrived today, my dear, and that you are feeling better. For now you can attend the ball and everyone can hear all the news you just shared with Miss Woodhouse and Miss Smith.

Scene 2

(A parlor at Hartfield about a week later. Mr. Woodhouse and Mr. Knightley are playing chess. Emma alternates between watching and wandering around the room.)

Mr. Knightley:
Mr. Woodhouse, how kind it was of you and Emma to have a party last night, welcoming Miss Fairfax to Highbury. It was a very pleasant evening, particularly when Emma and Miss Fairfax played the pianoforte. I'm glad you made her play so much, Emma; for having no instrument at her grandmother's it must have been a real indulgence for her..

Emma:
(slightly sarcastic)

I am happy you approved, but I hope I am not often so deficient in what is due to guests at Hartfield?

Mr. Woodhouse:
No, my dear! That I am sure you are not. There is nobody half so attentive as you.

Mr. Knightley:

No, you are not often deficient, either in manner or comprehension. I think, therefore, that you understand me.

Emma:

(slightly superior)

I understand you well enough.

(pause)

Miss Fairfax is reserved.

Mr. Knightley:

Are you saying you did not have a pleasant evening?

Emma:

Oh, no! I was pleased with my own perseverance in asking Miss Fairfax questions and amused to think how little information I obtained.

(realizes how she sounds and changes her tone)

I believe Miss Fairfax is an elegant young lady. I am sorry, however, that the Bates' circumstances are such that Miss Fairfax will surely be relegated to finding a position as a governess. I know that here at Hartfield Mrs. Weston was made to feel as one of the family; however, I realize that is not always the case with governesses.

Mr. Woodhouse:

Then we must do something to help them. I know! Emma, now that we have killed a porker, why do you not send a hind-quarter to the Bates. Whenever I speak with Mrs. Bates, she tells me how much she prefers pork.

Emma:

(smiles)

You are so kind, Father. I will do so today.

Mr. Woodhouse:

Ah, my dear; a note arrived for you while you were talking with Cook.

(hands her the note.)

Emma:

Thank you, Father.

(opens it and scans it)

It is from dear Mrs. Weston and she has the best of news. A letter arrived from Mr. Frank Churchill; he is to be arriving before the week's end.

Mr. Knightley:

Emma, I have another piece of news that I think will interest you.

Emma:

Oh?

Mr. Knightley:

Mr. Elton is to be married.

Emma:

What? How did you hear of it?

Mr. Knightley:

I was with Mr. Cole on business earlier today and he had just received a letter from Mr. Elton. Mr. Cole showed me the letter. It was short, but cheerful. I forget the precise words, but in short, it stated that he had been fortunate to win the hand of a Miss Hawkins.

Emma:

(not able to speak for a moment. Tries to be light)

Mr. Elton to be married? He will have everybody's wishes for his happiness.

Mr. Knightley:

(pauses)

Not…everybody's…I think.

Emma:

(looks at him)

No…you are correct.

(pause)

This is all so sudden. It cannot have been a very long acquaintance. He has been gone only four weeks.

(Harriet enters, appearing agitated.)

(Ad lib greetings)

Emma:
Harriet. I was afraid the rain might detain you.

Mr. Woodhouse:
You walked *in the rain?* My dear Miss Smith, Mr. Perry assures me that nothing is more disastrous to your health than breathing in *wet air*. Emma, pray pour Miss Smith a cup of tea.

(Emma crosses to the tea table, pours a cup of tea and brings it back to Harriet while the conversation continues.)

Harriet:
It was only a light mist when I started walking to Highbury, Mr. Woodhouse.

(wringing her hands, looking at Emma and then at the gentlemen and then at Emma.)

Mr. Knightley:

(noticing Harriet's state, crosses to Mr. Woodhouse)

Come, sir; let us retire to your study. I believe Harriet wishes to have a chat with Emma on a topic that we men would not appreciate.

Mr. Woodhouse:
Oh? Ah, good idea, Mr. Knightley. Miss Smith, pray move closer to the fire until your clothes are sufficiently dry.

Harriet:

(moves to sit near the fireplace)

Thank you, Mr. Woodbury; I shall.

(After Mr. Knightley and Mr. Woodhouse exit, Harriet jumps up and rushes to Emma.)

Harriet:
Oh, Miss Woodhouse, what do you think has happened?

Emma:

(gently)

I'm assuming you are speaking of Mr. Elton's engagement?

Harriet:

(shocked)

Mr. Elton? Engaged?

Emma:
Oh my dear, Harriet, forgive me. Mr. Knightley just gave us the news and when you entered, your agitation led me to think you had heard the news as well.

Harriet:

(pause)

As Mr. Elton did not want me, I cannot suppose he did not want any wife.

(takes a deep breath)

I wish him happiness.

Emma:

That is a kind and brave thing to say, my dear Harriet. But if your news was not about Mr. Elton, what was it about?

Harriet:

(recalls her news, agitated again)

It happened on my way here. It was a light mist when I left Mrs. Goddard's, but by the time I reached the village, the rain had turned quite heavy. I realized I could not go on and took shelter in Mr. Ford's haberdasher's shop. Who should already be in Mr. Ford's but Elizabeth Martin and her brother! Dear Miss Woodhouse, I thought I should have fainted. Elizabeth saw me directly and came to speak with me. She was quite friendly; she shook hands and asked how I did. I do not even remember what I answered.

By this time, the rain was letting up and I left. I got no more than three yards from the door, when Mr. Martin called my name. He was so polite and concerned with my getting wet. He suggested I go round by Mr. Cole's stables, as it was closer to Hartfield that way.

Miss Woodhouse! When I first saw him, I confess I was apprehensive; but there was a satisfaction in seeing him behave so pleasantly and kindly. Oh Miss Woodhouse, do talk to me and make me comfortable again!

Emma:

My dear Harriet, what passed was a mere trifle and quite unworthy of being dwelt on. It might be distressing for the moment, but you seem to have behaved extremely well. Now that it is over, and may never - *can never* – happen again, you need not think about it further.

Scene 3

(The parlor at Hartfield. Mr. Woodhouse, Mr. Weston and Mr. Frank Churchill are seated.)

Mr. Woodhouse:
I know your father and new mama-in-law are pleased to have you here. They have looked forward to you coming for some time.

Mr. Churchill:
And I have looked forward to being here.

(Emma enters the room.)

Emma:
Oh!

(stops)

Hello Mr. Weston. I did not know you had arrived.

(Mr. Weston and Mr. Churchill stand)

Mr. Weston:
We had arrived only a few minutes ago, my dear Miss Woodhouse. Pray let me introduce you to my son, Mr. Frank Churchill.

(ad lib greeting/curtsies/bows and then all sit)

Mr. Churchill:
I see that I owe Mrs. Weston an apology.

Emma:
Oh?

Mr. Churchill:
Yes. She spoke of your beauty, but I assumed her praise was from long acquaintance and partiality. Now I see she spoke the truth.

Emma:
You are too kind, Mr. Churchill.

Mr. Weston:
Handsomely said, Frank.

Mr. Churchill:
I understand that you are responsible for my father's happiness. You were most gracious to give up your Miss Taylor to allow her to become Mrs. Weston.

Mr. Weston:
That she was, Frank.

Mr. Churchill:
And this was another area where my assumptions proved wrong. I attributed my father's praises of Mrs. Weston to the affection of a groom. I was prepared for an elegant lady with agreeable manners, but I confess I had not expected to find my father's wife to be a beauty.

Emma:
You cannot see too much perfection in Mrs. Weston for my part.

Mr. Weston:
(stands)

I must really be going. I have business at the Crown and have several errands for Mrs. Weston at Fords.

Mr. Churchill:
(stands)

As you are going farther on business, sir, I will take the opportunity of paying a visit which must be paid some time or other and therefore might as well be today. I have the honor of being acquainted with a neighbor of yours, Miss Woodhouse. There is a lady residing in Highbury, whose grandmother is the widow of the former vicar; Barnes or Bates. Do you know any family of that name?

Mr. Woodhouse:
To be sure we do, if the young lady of whom you speak is Miss Fairfax. Mrs. Bates is her grandmother and Miss Bates her aunt. She is a very agreeable young lady. Her grandmamma and aunt are very worthy people and will be extremely glad to see you.

Mr. Weston:
That's right, Frank; you are acquainted with Miss Fairfax. You knew her at Weymouth. Call upon her today, by all means. Do not defer it. What is right to be done cannot be done too soon.

(Mr. Weston turns to speak to Mr. Woodhouse leaving Emma and Mr. Churchill to speak with each other.)

Mr. Churchill:
Yes, I can claim slight acquaintance with Miss Fairfax, although most of my knowledge of her comes from reports of other people.

(pause)

I understand she is a quiet and elegant young lady.

Emma:
I must say, Mr. Churchill, that if you were never particularly struck by her manners before, I think you will be today. You will see her to advantage; see her and hear no…no, I am afraid you will not *hear* her at all, for she has an aunt who never holds her tongue.

Mr. Weston:
(turns back to them)

Come then, Frank; let us be gone.

Mr. Churchill:
Mr. Woodhouse, it was a pleasure to meet you, Sir.

Mr. Woodhouse:
And you as well, Mr. Churchill. Pray come and see us often while you are in Highbury.

Mr. Churchill:
Thank you, sir.

Mr. Weston:
Miss Woodhouse, it's always a pleasure to see you.

Emma:
And you as well, Mr. Weston. Pray give my best to Mrs. Weston and tell her I look forward to talking with her at the Cole's party.

Mr. Weston:
I will tell her. When Mrs. Cole hear that Frank was expected by the week's end, she was kind enough to extend an invitation for Frank to attend at well.

Emma:
How kind of her. Then I will see you tomorrow night, Mr. Churchill.

Mr. Churchill:
You will. (He takes her hand and kisses it.) And I look forward to getting to know you better, Miss Woodhouse.

Scene 4

(A parlor at the Cole's house. A pianoforte is in the corner. Mr. and Mrs. Cole are greeting guests as they arrive: Mr. and Mrs. Weston, Frank Churchill, Mrs. Bates, Miss Bates, Jane Fairfax, Mrs. Goddard, Harriet Smith, Mr. Knightley and Emma.)

Mrs. Cole:
Good evening, Miss Woodhouse. It was so good of you to come to our party.

Emma:
Good evening, Mrs. Cole, Mr. Cole. It was so kind of you to invite me.

Mrs. Cole:
My dear Miss Woodhouse, I'm sure you have heard the news of Mr. Elton's being engaged?

Emma:
Yes, ma'am, I have. Father and I wish them both much happiness.

Mrs. Cole:
I understand that we will have that pleasure soon. Mr. Elton wrote Mr. Cole that, within a fortnight he plans to return to Highbury with his new bride.

Emma:
I look forward to meeting his wife. Highbury will be bursting with newcomers.

Mrs. Cole:
(looks around to make sure no one is listening)

Speaking of newcomers, have you heard about the news about Miss Fairfax?

Emma:
No, I have not.

Mrs. Cole:
I called on Miss Bates yesterday morning and when I entered their parlor, there stood an elegant little pianoforte. Miss Bates informed me that the instrument had arrived the day before as a gift for Jane. They were all quite bewildered to think who could possibly have sent it, but tonight I have my suspicions.

(looks around again)

I believe it is Mr. Knightley.

Emma:
Mr. Knightley?

Mr. Cole:
My dear, Mrs. Goddard has been looking for you.

Mrs. Cole:
I'll come immediately, my dear. Pardon me, Miss Woodhouse

(cross the room)

(Mr. Knightley crosses to her.)

Mr. Knightley:
Good evening, Emma.

Emma:
Ah, Mr. Knightley, I see you have come in your coach, like a proper gentlemen should, rather than walking.

Mr. Knightley:
Well, there is a reason for the carriage tonight.

(Mrs. Bates, Miss Bates and Jane Fairfax cross to her)

Miss Bates:
Good evening, Miss Woodhouse, how lovely to see you tonight. Is Mr. Woodhouse with you?

Emma:
Good evening, Miss Bates, Mrs. Bates. No, Father is not with me tonight. He does not like to travel abroad after dark; Mr. Perry warns against the night air.

Miss Bates:
I completely understand. Mr. Perry warns against the night air for

Mother as well. In fact, we would not have been able to come at all, had not dear Mr. Knightley been so kind as to offer to bring us in his coach. You rescued us from a lonely evening.

(giggles to Emma)

Mr. Knightley was truly our *knight;*

(turns to Mrs. Bates)

was he not Mother?

Mrs. Bates:
Pork!

Miss Bates:
Not pork, Mother. Mrs. Cole told me that she is serving a lovely fowl dish tonight.

(to Emma)

I saw Mr. Knightley riding down the street yesterday and I called to him to come and see Jane's new pianoforte - someone has been so kind as to send a lovely little pianoforte to Jane; we think it's the Campbells, but as there was no card with the delivery, we may never know. Anyhow, when Mr. Knightley stepped in to admire the instrument, he learned of our dilemma concerning transportation and offered to bring us tonight in his carriage. He was even so kind as to arrange for a hot brick, wrapped in flannel, to place under our feet. We were so warm and toasty all the way here.

Mr. Knightley:
It was my pleasure, ma'am.

Emma:
Mr. Knightley is always attentive.

Miss Bates:
If you will excuse me, Mrs. Cole offered to set a chair near the

fireplace for Mother.

(Miss Bates and Mrs. Bates cross the room. Mr. and Mrs. Weston and Mr. Churchill cross. Ad lib greetings.)

Emma:
How are you enjoying your visit, Mr. Churchill?

Mr. Churchill:
I am enjoying it immensely, Miss Woodhouse. Between Father and my Mama-in-law I have met all the inhabitants of Highbury, been to my father's office, to the Crown Inn, to Mr. Ford's haberdasher shop, and to Mr. Down's bakery shop.

Emma:
Then you have seen just about everything there is to see in Highbury.

Mrs. Weston:
We also stopped in at the Bateses, for Mr. Churchill assured me that I had told Miss Bates that I would come. I do not recall it, but we had a lovely visit. We talked for length about how fortunate it is that Mr. Churchill will be able to attend the ball.

Mr. Weston:
Speaking of Miss Bates, my dear, I see her beckoning to us. We should go and speak to her and her mother. Excuse us, Miss Woodhouse.

(They cross to Miss Bates, leaving Mr. Churchill and Emma alone.)

Emma:
So you were able to renew your acquaintance with Miss Fairfax?

Mr. Churchill:
Yes, oh, yes! I saw all three ladies, and was very obliged to you for your *preparatory* hint. If the talking aunt had taken me by

surprise, it might have been the death of me. By the time the good lady paused to draw breath, she had been talking very nearly three quarters of an hour.

(laughs)

Emma:

(laughs quietly)

And how do you think Miss Fairfax looking?

Mr. Churchill:

Ill—that is, if a young lady can ever be allowed to look ill. Miss Fairfax is naturally so pale, as to almost give the appearance of ill health. A deplorable want of complexion. And so reserved.

(paused, suddenly solemn)

But that may be a positive thing in her situation.

Emma:

As you knew her at Weymouth, I assume that you know Miss Fairfax's situation in life; that her aunt and grandmother are unable to provide for her future and she is destined to find a position as a governess?

Mr. Churchill:

Yes…I believe I do.

Mrs. Cole:

(crosses to Emma)

Miss Woodhouse, I require your assistance.

Emma:

I will be most happy to help you, Mrs. Cole.

Mrs. Cole:

I have been attempting to persuade Miss Fairfax to play the pianoforte for us, for we all know from Miss Bates that she is quite an accomplished pianist. However, being new to Highbury, Miss Fairfax is hesitant to play in company. I assured her she would not be alone in her performance, as I felt certain I could call upon you to play for us first.

Emma:
Oh, well…

(sees there is no way to get out of it)

Very well.

(Mrs. Cole leads her to the pianoforte, while everyone else sits down or finds a place to lean against the wall to listen. Emma plays and sings a simple love song; in the last chorus, Mr. Churchills stands up and sings with her, crossing to stand by the instrument. When it's over, everyone applauds and congratulates them.)

Mrs. Cole:
Thank you, Miss Woodhouse, Mr. Churchill. You see, Miss Fairfax, there is no need to be shy; please do us the honor of hearing you play.

(Miss Fairfax crosses to the pianoforte and plays. Emma sits. Mr. Knightley joins her.)

Mr. Knightley:
That was very well done, Emma.

Emma:
Thank you, Mr. Knightley.

(she sees him smiling as he watches Miss Fairfax play)

Miss Bates was correct; Miss Fairfax is an accomplished pianist.

Mr. Knightley:
Yes, she is.

Emma:
How kind of…*the Campbells*…to give Miss Fairfax a pianoforte. I understand she was quite surprised.

Mr. Knightley:
Surprises are foolish things. The pleasure is not enhanced and the inconvenience is often considerable. It was bad judgment on Colonel Campbell's part.

(They listen to Miss Fairfax finish the song. Everyone applauds.)

Mr. Churchill:
Miss Fairfax, I think you could manage another song without effort.

Mr. Knightley:
(indignantly, speaking so that only Emma hears)

That fellow thinks of nothing but his own pleasure.

(gets up and crosses to Miss Bates)

Miss Bates, you must do something; Jane will sing herself hoarse.

Miss Bates:
Oh my, yes of course.

(Mr. Knightley and Miss Bates cross to Jane; quiet conversation goes on. Mrs. Weston crosses to sit next to Emma.)

Mrs. Weston:
I understand that Mr. Knightley conveyed the Bateses and Miss Fairfax in his carriage. What a kind attention.

Emma:
Yes, he is a humane man. See but how concerned he is of Miss

Fairfax's health.

Mrs. Weston:
You give him credit for a simple disinterested benevolence, but a suspicion entered my head and I have not been able to get it out. In fact, the more I think of it, the more probable it appears. In short, it appears that an attachment between Mr. Knightley and Miss Fairfax might be growing.

Emma:
An attachment? Between Mr. Knightley and Miss Fairfax?

(laughs)

How could you think such a thing? Mr. Knightley does not want to marry; I am sure he has not the least idea of it. You have taken up an idea, Mrs. Weston, and run away with it, as you have many a time reproached me with doing. I see no sign of attachment – I believe nothing of the rumor that the pianoforte is from him – and only proof shall convince me that Mr. Knightley has any thought of marrying Jane Fairfax.

(looks over and sees Mr. Knightley talking with Miss Fairfax. She is smiling at him.)

He...cannot...be thinking...of...marriage...surely...not...

(She looks at Mrs. Weston, who smiles.)

Scene 5

(The parlor at Hartfield several weeks later. Emma enters.)

Emma:
Ah Mr. Churchill, how do you do?

Mr. Churchill:
I am well, Miss Woodhouse; and yourself?

Emma:
I am well. Will you have some tea?

Mr. Churchill:
I am sorry, but I cannot. In fact, I have come to say goodbye.

Emma:
Goodbye? Surely you are not leaving?

Mr. Churchill:
I am afraid I must. A letter arrived this morning from my aunt. She is far from well and needs me immediately. I am uncertain of when I shall return to Highbury.

Emma:
I am sorry to hear of Mrs. Churchill's poor health. When do you leave?

Mr. Churchill:
Within the hour. I have been paying calls on those here in Highbury whom I feel have become…more than kind acquaintances.

(pauses, moody, deep in thought)

Of all horrid things, leave-taking is the worst.

Emma:
Your presence will be missed at the ball.

Mr. Churchill:
The ball! Perhaps I will be back in time. My father depends on it. You must promise me the first dance.

(pause)

Such a fortnight it has been. Every day more precious and delightful than the day before.

(he takes her hand)

Ah, Miss Woodhouse, I am certain that you may suspect; but my regard for Highbury – and *certain* of its inhabitants – has grown most warm. You, Miss Woodhouse have…

(Mr. Weston enters and interrupts them. Emma pulls her hand out of Mr. Churchill's grasp.)

Mr. Weston:
Good afternoon, Miss Woodhouse. Frank, we must leave soon.

Mr. Churchill:
Of course, Father.

(to Emma)

I have engaged Mrs. Weston's promise to correspond with me. Through her, it shall almost be as if I am at dear Highbury again.

(he takes her hand and kisses it.)

Goodbye for now, Miss Woodhouse.

(Mr. Churchill and Mr. Weston exit. Emma stands spellbound, touching the spot on her hand where he kissed it. Speaks to herself.)

Emma:
Mr. Churchill loves me.

(wonderingly)

And, as I feel this sensation of listlessness, I must be in love with him.

(frowns)

I confess I expected love to feel different.

(takes a deep breath)

I am certain his absence will confirm the depth of my feeling.

Scene 6

(The parlor at Hartfield the next day. Emma and Mr. Woodhouse, Mr. Elton and Mrs. Elton, Mr. Knightley, Miss Bates, Miss Fairfax, Mr. Weston and Mrs. Weston. The men are talking quietly to each other as are the other ladies, leaving Emma to speak with Mrs. Elton)

Mrs. Elton:
I vow, Hartfield reminds me my brother's estate.

(turns to Mr. Elton)

Does it not remind you of Maple Grove, Mr. E.?

(He turns to respond, but she ignores him and continues)

Mrs. Elton:
Very like Maple Grove indeed. Why this room is the very shape and size of the morning-room at Maple Grove; I could almost fancy myself at Maple Grove.

(turns to Mr. Elton)

Do you not fancy yourself at Maple Grove, Mr. E.?

(He turns to respond, but she ignores him and continues)

Mrs. Elton:
My brother and sister will be enchanted with this place. People who have extensive grounds themselves are always pleased with other places that have extensive grounds.

Emma:
I am certain that Surry is full of beautiful places.

Mrs. Elton:
Oh, yes, I am quite aware of that. It is the garden of England, you know.

Emma:
Many counties, I believe, are called the garden of England.

Mrs. Elton:
No, I fancy not. I have never heard any county, but Surry called so.

(looks towards Mr. Woodhouse and then lowers her voice to talk to Emma)

But then, I understand from Mr. E. that your father's heath is a great drawback to you. Let me recommend Bath to you; I have no doubt it will do Mr. Woodhouse good.

Emma:
My father tried it more than once, but without receiving any benefit.

Mrs. Elton:
That is a pity, for if he were to go to Bath, then I could secure you some of the best society in the place. A line from me would bring you a host of acquaintances.

(Emma turns and takes a sip of tea to keep from saying something she would regret. After a moment, she turns back to Mrs. Elton.)

Emma:
Are you musical, Mrs. Elton?

Mrs. Elton:
I am fond of music – passionately fond – and my friends say that I am not entirely devoid of taste. I cannot do without music. When Mr. E. was speaking of my future home, I said that two carriages were not necessary to my happiness, nor were large, spacious

rooms – although I had grown quite accustomed to them – but without music, life would be a blank to me.

In fact, Miss Woodhouse, you and I must establish a musical club and have weekly meeting at your house or ours.

(pauses to look towards the Westons and lowers her voice)

Mr. E and I called at Randalls this morning. Mr. Weston seems an excellent creature – quite first rate with me already, I assure you. And Mrs. Weston…I was astonished to find her so very lady-like; I understand she was your governess?

Emma:

(slightly heated)

Mrs. Weston's manners were always particularly good. Their propriety, simplicity and elegance would make them the safest model for any young woman.

Mrs. Elton:

(ignores Emma's tone. Notices Jane Fairfax talking with Mrs. Weston)

I also met Mrs. Bates, Miss Bates and Jane Fairfax. I quite rave about Jane Fairfax. What a sweet and talented young lady. Her situation is calculated to affect one. I understand from Mr. E. that she can expect nothing from her grandmother and aunt. Miss Woodhouse, we must exert ourselves and endeavor to do something for her. As the first ladies of Highbury, it is our responsibility to help Jane Fairfx.

Emma:

I would not say she has nothing…Colonel and Mrs. Campbell -

Mrs. Elton:

(interrupts)

Ah, my dear Miss Woodhouse, whatever advantages she may have enjoyed with the Campbells are at an end. I believe that a vast deal may be done by those who act. If *we* set the example, many will follow. As for her having to take any position offered to her, *my* acquaintances is so very extensive, that I have little doubt of hearing of something to suit her shortly.

(Mrs. Elton's quiets down enough to hear Miss Fairfax speaking to Mr. Woodhouse.)

Miss Fairfax:

I look forward to the ball. I met Mrs. Cole when I was returning from the post office this morning and we spoke about it at length.

Mr. Woodhouse:

I am sorry to hear of your being in the rain. Young ladies should take care of themselves, for they are like delicate plants.

Mrs. Elton:

(interrupts the conversation)

What? Going to the post-office in the rain? My dear Jane, this must not be. How could you do such a thing? It is a sign that I was not there to take care of you.

Miss Fairfax:

You need not be worried, Mrs. Elton, for I am fine.

Mrs. Elton:

Oh, do not tell me. You really are a sad girl, and do not know how to take care of yourself. I will speak to Mr. E. The man who fetches our letters shall enquire for your's too and bring them to you.

Miss Fairfax:

You are extremely kind, but I cannot give up my early walk.

Mrs. Elton:

My dear Jane, say no more about it, the thing is determined.

(turns and looks for Mr. Knightley)

Knightley! Knightley! Pray, use you influence to encourage Jane to care for herself.

Mr. Knightley:
Mrs. Elton, although we all care about Jane's health, why should she give attention to my encouragement?

(Awkward silence, until Mrs. Weston tries to ease it.)

Mrs. Weston:
Speaking of letters, Emma, did I tell you that we heard from Mr. Churchill this morning? He writes to say that he will be returning in time for our ball. I brought his letter, thinking you might enjoy reading his description of Enscombe.

(She takes a letter out of her bag and extends it to Emma, but Mrs. Elton walks up and takes it instead.)

Mrs. Elton:
I have heard all about Mr. Churchill from Mr. E.

(she scans the letter)

and of Enscombe. I understand it is sixty-five miles to London; but what is distance to people of large fortune? Mr. Churchill writes a pleasant enough letter. What a beautiful hand; it is one of the best of any man's writing I have ever seen.

(hands the letter to Mr. Knightley)

Do you not agree, Knightley?

Mr. Knightley:
(glances at the letter without reading it)

I do not admire it.

(He extends the letter, Mrs. Elton tries to take it and Mr. Knightley lifts it away from her grasp and gives it to Mrs. Weston)

It is too small and wants strength. It is like a woman's writing.

(Awkward silence again, until Emma announces)

Emma:
Shall we all go in to supper?

(Everyone turns to walk through the door. Mrs. Elton walks up to Mr. Woodhouse.)

Mrs. Elton:
Must I go first? All this attention given me; I really am ashamed of always leading the way. Miss Fairfax, later we must speak of finding you a position. I have already written several letters to my friends, inquiring whether they knew of a family requiring a governess.

(They exit in pairs, leaving Emma by herself.)

Emma:
I am not in love; I no longer feel any fluttering whenever Mr. Churchill's name is mentioned. Yet, how will I feel when I see him at the ball?

Mr. Knightley:
(returns to the room)

Emma? Are you coming?

Emma:
What? Oh! Yes.

(she takes his extended arm.)

I was merely thinking aloud about the Weston's ball. Will you attend?

Mr. Knightley:
No. I have no taste for dancing and I can think of nothing appealing about standing about watching other people dance.

(They exit.)

Scene 7

(The ball at the assembly hall in Highbury. Mr. Cole, Mrs. Cole, Mr. Weston, Mrs. Weston, Mr. Churchill and Mr. Knightley are already there. Emma, Mrs. Goddard and Harriet enter. Mr. Churchill crosses to meet them. Ad lib greetings, curtsies/bows. Harriet and Mrs. Goddard cross to greet other people.)

Emma:
Mr. and Mrs. Weston were anxious that you arrive in time for the ball.

Mr. Churchill:
I was determined to be here in time and left earlier this morning. Come, I promised Mrs. Weston that I would bring you to her the moment you arrived.

(They cross to Mrs. Weston. Ad lib greetings.)

Emma:
It appears that all of Highbury is here tonight.

Mrs. Weston:
Yes, it is a great comfort to Mr. Weston. He has been most anxious that this be a wonderful evening.

(laughs)

Indeed he has asked many people to arrive early, in order to give their opinion on the room's decorations.

Mr. Churchill:
Yet, not *all* of Highbury is here. I do not see the *quiet* Miss Bates

and Miss Fairfax.

Mrs. Weston:
Mr. Churchill!

(they laugh)

Well, Miss Bates has little to do with her day and she harms no one.

Mr. Churchill:
Harms no one? I must disagree with you, ma'am. Miss Bates harms my ears after only half an hour in her company.

(he laughs)

Mrs. Weston:
Mr. Churchill, remember your manners! Miss Fairfax *and* Miss Bates – along with her mother – are coming with Mr. and Mrs. Elton.

Mr. Churchill:
Ah, at last I will meet the famous Mrs. Elton. If you ladies will excuse me, I will watch for their arrival. Miss Woodhouse, Father and Mrs. Weston told me how *concerned* Mrs. Elton was over Miss Fairfax's health. I will stand at the door with an umbrella ready, to prevent Miss Fairfax from coming in contact with even *one* drop of rain. *That* should satisfy Mrs. Elton.

(He grins and exits.)

Mrs. Weston:
I'm afraid Mr. Churchill is being mischievous at Mrs. Elton's expense.

Emma:
Yet it is difficult not to join in the laughter.

(Mr. Elton, Mrs. Elton, Miss Bates, Miss Fairfax and Mr. Churchill enter.)

Miss Bates:

So very obliging of you, Mr. Churchill. I didn't feel a drop of rain. Not that I care for myself. My shoes are quite thick. But Jane's…

(notices the room)

Well, this is brilliant indeed. Excellently contrived upon my word. Did you ever see anything like it? I will tell Mother all about it when we arrive home. She is spending the evening with Mr. Woodhouse. Mr. Churchill, I must tell you that my mother's spectacles have never been in fault since you replaced the rivet. Mother often speaks of your good nature, does she not, Jane? How do you do, Miss Woodhouse, Mrs. Weston? I am well, thank you. I hope you are quite well. We are so happy to be here tonight. Does Jane not look lovely? Her gown was a gift from Colonel and Mrs. Campbell; was that not kind? And she dressed her own hair.You and Mr. Weston have turned this room into a fairy-land. And dear Mrs. Elton and Mr. Elton were so obliging as too offer us a most comfortable carriage ride. There is Mrs. Goddard; if you will excuse me, I will go and speak to them.

(She crosses the room to leave the others to make ad lib greetings bows/curtsies)

Mrs. Elton:

Mrs. Weston, the decorations in the room are quite nice. It rather reminds me of when my brother and his wife held a reception in their smaller parlor.

Mrs. Weston:

Uh…thank you, Mrs. Elton.

Emma:

Miss Fairfax, you look lovely tonight.

Miss Fairfax:

As do you, Miss Woodhouse.

Mrs. Elton

(unhappy about the lack of attention, speaks

quickly)

Nobody can think less of dress in general than I do, but upon such an occasion as this, when everybody's eyes are so much upon me – and in compliment to the Westons – who I have no doubt are giving this ball chiefly to do me honor – I would not wish to be inferior to others. And I see very few pearls in the room except mine. Mr. Churchill, I understand that you are a capital dancer. We shall see if our styles suit. Ah, you must excuse me, for I see Mrs. Cole and must go and compliment her on the delicious cakes she baked for us last week. Come, my dear Jane; I have heard from my friends and want to tell you about the prospects for you they have shared.

(They cross the room.)

Mrs. Weston:
If you will excuse me, I must see if the musicians are ready for dancing.

(she exits the room)

Emma:

(softly, so as to not be overheard)

How do you like Mrs. Elton?

Mr. Churchill:
Not at all. What can she mean about whether our styles suit?

Emma:
Well, I imagine since she considers herself the guest of honor, she would expect to begin the ball with you as her partner.

Mr. Churchill:
Well, I cannot, for you promised me a dance, did you not? Mrs. Elton can dance with my father.

(Music beings and partners form the lines. Emma dances with Mr. Churchill, Mr. Weston with Mrs.

Elton and Mr. Cole with Mrs. Cole. Mr. Knightley is in the corner, watching. Mrs. Weston and Mrs. Goddard are sitting on another side, watching and whispering. Harriet is sitting nearby with Miss Bates. Mr. Elton wanders around, watching the dancers.

Emma notices that Harriet is not dancing and looks over at Mrs. Weston and nods her head at Harriet. Mrs. Weston gets the message and nods back. Mr. Elton walks up to Mrs. Weston and Mrs. Goddard.)

Mrs. Weston:
Mr. Elton, do you not dance?

Mr. Elton:
Most readily, Mrs. Weston, if you will dance with me.

Mrs. Weston:
Me! Oh, no. I would get you a better partner than myself. I am no dancer.

Mr. Elton:
Then, if Mrs. Goddard wishes to dance, I shall have great pleasure, I am sure. For though beginning to feel myself rather an old married man – and my dancing days are over – it would give me great pleasure to stand up with an old friend like Mrs. Goddard.

Mrs. Goddard:
Oh, no, Mr. Elton, you would not wish to dance with one my age when there are others.

Mrs. Weston:
Yes, there is a young lady who I should be very glad to see dancing. Miss Smith.

Mr. Elton:
Miss Smith…oh…I had not observed. You are extremely

obliging…and if I were not an old married man…but my dancing days are over. If you will excuse me, Mrs. Weston, Mrs. Goddard.

(Emma sees him walk away, catches his wife's eye – they share a triumphant glance – and he crosses towards Mr. Knightley. Harriet overheard the conversation and lowers her head, trying to fight off tears. Right before Mr. Elton reaches Mr. Knightley, Mr. Knightley crosses to Harriet and extends his hand, asking her to dance. Her face is radiant as she takes his hand and they join the dance.

After the dance, other people change partners. Mrs. Elton walks over to talk with Mr. Elton, looking haughtily around the room. Emma crosses to a quiet corner and Mr. Knightley joins her.)

Emma:
Thank you, Mr. Knightley. That was most kind of you.

Mr. Knightley:
Mr. Elton's rudeness was unpardonable…and his wife…Their aim was clearly to wound not just Harriet, but also you for, I suspect, that you wished him to marry Harriet.

Emma:
I did and, for that, they cannot forgive me.

(pause)

I do own myself to have been completely mistaken in Mr. Elton. There is a littleness about him which you discovered and which I did not. I was fully convinced of his being in love with Harriet.

Mr. Knightley:
I will do you justice to say that you would have chosen for him better than he chose for himself. Harriet Smith has some finer

qualities which Mrs. Elton lacks. I found Harriet more conversable than I expected.

Mr. Weston:
(crosses to them)

Come, Miss Woodhouse, it is time for the last dance.

Emma:
I am ready, Sir.

Mr. Knightley:
Whom are you going to dance with?

Emma:
(pauses)

With you, if you will ask me.

Mr. Knightley:
(extends his hand)

Will you?

Emma:
Indeed I will.

(takes his hand)

You have shown that you can dance and you know we are not really so much brother and sister as to make it at all improper.

Mr. Knightley:
(smiles)

Brother and sister! No, indeed!

Scene 8

(A garden at Hartfield. Emma is sitting on a bench, writing in her diary.)

Emma:

Dear Diary, Altogether, the ball turned out to be quite delightful, with several things lending themselves to its success. The impertinence of the Eltons threatened to ruin the evening, but it opened Harriet's eyes to see that Mr. Elton was not the superior man she believed him to be.

It appears that Frank Churchill is not as in love with me as I had earlier supposed. That is a relief, as I did not wish to hurt him. I return to my former condition of being quite content never to marry.

Being back on good terms with Mr. Knightley gave me considerable pleasure, I left the ball with a warm, golden glow.

(Mr. Woodhouse enters. Emma closes her diary.)

Mr. Woodhouse:

Ah, there you are my dear. I wish I could convince you not to go on this outing today. I am concerned for your safety.

Emma:

Father, there is nothing harmful in a party to pick strawberries, unless we harm our appetites from eating too many berries.

Mr. Woodhouse:

I am referring to the gypsies that attacked Miss Smith last week.

Emma:

It was frightening for Harriet – and indeed for all of us living in Highbury. To think of her walking only half a mile away from Highbury when those gypsies set upon her.

Mr. Woodhouse:

Poor Miss Smith; I'm certain she was terrified.

Emma:

She was. She told me she promised them money, and took out her purse, which I believe only worsened the situation.

Mr. Woodhouse:
I do not want to think what would have occurred had Mr. Churchill not happened upon the scene and come to her rescue. I wish you would reconsider…what if the gypsies are still lingering in the area?

Emma:
Father, pray do not worry. When Mr. Knightley heard of it, he led a group of men to inspect the area surrounding Highbury. There was no sign of the gypsies. But to put you at ease, let me remind you that our party today will include Mr. Elton, Mr. Churchill and Mr. Knightley. Certainly no gypsies would consider approaching, much less accosting, a group such as ours.

Mr. Woodhouse:
You're right, my dear. Pray forgive an old man his fears for a beloved daughter. I do not know what I would do without you.

Emma:
(crosses and kisses his cheek)

Nor do you have to worry, for I assure you that nothing will take me away from you.

Mr. Woodhouse:
Well, it is time for my tonic and nap. Mr. Perry insists that I am punctual with both.

Emma:
Then you must go immediately. If you would be so kind as to carry my diary and pen indoors, I must go and meet Harriet; we are walking together to meet the others.

(she hands him her diary.)

Mr. Woodhouse:
Have a good time then, my dear and I'll see you at supper.

Emma:
Goodbye Father.

(She places a bonnet on her head and picks up a basket and walks towards Harriet who is crossing to her. Ad lib greetings.)

Emma:
I am looking forward to today; strawberries are my one of my favorites.

Harriet:
Mine as well; I promised Mrs. Goddard I would pick enough for her to bake pies.

(pauses)

Miss Woodhouse, before we join the others, there is something I need to tell you…I know we shall have a certain couple in our group today and I wanted to assure you that my feelings…I am ashamed…how could I for so long a time fancy myself in love…I see nothing at all extraordinary in him now. I do not envy his wife nor do I admire her. No, let them be happy together. In my heart there is an end to Mr. Elton.

Emma:
I am glad to hear you say this, Harriet. For when you do marry, you would not want a husband wondering about…

Harriet:
I shall never marry.

Emma:
Never? Surely this conviction is not a compliment to Mr. Elton?

Harriet:
Mr. Elton! Oh no!

(pauses, slowly, as if hinting)

There are other men who are vastly superior to Mr. Elton!

Emma:
Harriet, I will not affect to be in doubt of your meaning. I

understand your resolution of never marrying results from an idea that the person whom you *prefer* you consider to be your superior in situation, is that not so?

Harriet:
Oh Miss Woodhouse, believe me I have not the presumption to suppose – indeed I am not so mad – but it is a pleasure to admire him from a distance. He is superior to all the rest of the world and my gratitude to him is infinite.

Emma:
I am not at all surprised. The service he rendered you was enough to warm your heart.

Harriet:
The very recollection of it still leaves me trembling. All the wretchedness I felt at the time and then I saw him coming. To think that in one moment I could change from perfect misery to perfect happiness.

Emma:
It is very natural and honorable. But, perhaps it would be wisest to keep your feelings in check for a time, until you are persuaded of his liking you. Be observant of him; let his behavior be the guide. I give you this caution now, because I am determined against all interference on my part. Let no name ever pass our lips. We were wrong before; we will be caution now. He is your superior in situation, but Harriet more wonderful things have taken place. There have been matches of greater disparity.

Harriet:
Oh, Miss Woodhouse! You have given me such hope! To imagine that Mr. –

Emma:
No! Do not speak his name. Now come; the others are waiting. There are strawberries to be picked!

Scene 9

(A field. Mr. Knightley, Miss Bates and Miss Fairfax are seated on one blanket. Harriet, Emma and Mr. Churchill on another. Mr. Elton and Mrs. Elton are seated one. There are several baskets around as well. General ad lib about gathering strawberries.)

Mr. Churchill:
Miss Woodhouse, how much I am obliged to you for telling me to come today. If it had not been for you, I should have lost all the happiness of this party.

Emma:
You are too kind, Mr. Churchill, for as you came late, you lost all the best strawberries.

Mr. Churchill:
But you saved me some.

Emma:
Yes, I am a kinder friend than you deserve and I know how much Mrs. Weston loves strawberries.

Mrs. Elton:
(cannot bear to be the center of attention and interrupts this conversation)

Ah, my dear Jane. I have found you a position in Bath! I heard from a cousin of my dear friend; a Mrs. Bragge. My friend assures me that Mrs. Bragge is delightful and charming, known in the first circles. She is most anxious to meet you and I told her I knew you would wish me to secure your position at once.

Miss Fairfax:
I am obliged, but I cannot consider leaving Highbury.

Mrs. Elton:
As your protector, I cannot allow you to feel. What are your options? I am sure you agree with me, Miss Bates, do you not, that this is best for Jane?

Miss Bates:
Well, I…

Mrs. Elton:
See! Your aunt is speechless with delight. I will write an acquiescence by tomorrow's post.

Miss Fairfax:
(sharply)

Aunt Bates, I am certain we have not gathered enough strawberries. You know how Grandmother loves them. Mr. Knightley, would you be so kind as to escort us to find more?

Mr. Knightley:
Certainly, Miss Fairfax.

(He helps both ladies to their feet. They exit. Awkward silence.)

Mrs. Elton:
Well, I am satisfied with the day. The weather is perhaps a bit warm for this time of year, but as you see, I have worn a large bonnet to shield my face. A lady cannot be too fastidious when it comes to protecting her complexion. What a darling little hat you are wearing, Miss Woodhouse.

Emma:
Thank you, Mrs. Elton.

Mrs. Elton:
I wish we had a donkey. It would have been just the thing to ride a donkey here. Mr. E., we must look into purchasing a donkey. In a country life, I conceive it to be a necessity.

Mr. Elton:
I know nothing about donkeys, but I will look into it.

Mrs. Elton:
Wonderful. I would like a chestnut donkey, as I think it would look charming against my riding habit. Mr. Churchill, how is your aunt? I understand her health has been poor of late.

Mr. Churchill:
Thank you for asking; my aunt's health is not as strong as we would like.

Mrs. Elton:
She should go to Bath and take the waters. Nowhere in all of England can you find waters with the healthful benefits like the waters of Bath. Surely she can go to Bath.

Mr. Churchill:
I cannot say –

Mrs. Elton:
Of course she can! And I will write a letter of introduction for her to all of my friends in Bath. With it she will be certain of a warm reception from those of the first society. I told Miss Woodhouse that if her father were to take the waters in Bath, he would recover his strength, but she insists he is perfectly content with Mr. Perry's care.

Emma:
My father –

Mrs. Elton:
What can be taking Jane so long?

(lifts her voice)

Jane! My dear girl, do come back.

(Miss Fairfax, Miss Bates and Mr. Knightley cross back towards them. Mrs. Elton lowers her voice to speak to those around her.)

Mrs. Elton:

I am certain that we found all the strawberries that were growing now. Jane needs to take her future in mind and guard her actions. While asking Knightley to escort her might be considered proper *for the present time*, when she is in service, that action would be frowned upon. I will do what I can to keep this information from reaching Mrs. Bragge; after all my efforts on her behalf, I would not want Jane losing such an advantageous position. Although young ladies of all stations must always be cautious of their reputation.

(lowers to voice to pretend to speak only to Emma, but everyone hears)

Which is why, Miss Woodhouse, you will be happy to take my advice about your behavior today in regards to Mr. Churchill. I am certain you believed the laughter and frivolity between you two were modest, but there are those who would consider it overt *flirting*!

(As she pauses a moment and the three sit back down, Mr. Churchill speaks quickly.)

Mr. Churchill:

A game! Ladies and gentlemen…let us have a game! I am ordered by Miss Woodhouse – who presides wherever she is – to say that she desires to know what you are all thinking.

Mr. Knightley:

Is Miss Woodhouse sure that she would like to hear what we are all thinking?

Emma:

No, no, no! Upon no account. Not everything. Say one or two

thoughts.

Mr. Churchill:
Then Miss Woodhouse requires from each of you either one thing very clever - be it prose or verse – or two things moderately clever, or three things very dull indeed and she will laugh heartily at them all.

Miss Bates:
(laughs)

Oh very well, That will do just for me, you know, for I shall be sure to say something dull as soon as ever I open my mouth.

Emma:
Ah, but there may be a difficulty, for you will be limited to only three.

(Dead silence, as everyone realizes what Emma said. Miss Bates' expression changes from innocent fun to realization of what Emma was saying.)

Miss Bates:
(looks away and lowers her voice; not anger, but embarrassed that she has been so foolish.)

Ah!...well…to be sure. Yes, I see what she means.

(turns to Mr. Knightley)

I will try to hold my tongue. I must make myself very disagreeable or she would not have said such a thing to an old friend.

Mr. Knightley:
I am not fond of games such as these. I would like to see the view.

(he stands and extends his hand to Miss Bates)

Miss Bates, would you do me the honor of walking with me?

(Miss Bates nods and takes his hand to stand. They exit.)

Mrs. Elton:
For myself, I protest I must be excused. I do not pretend to be a wit, I have a great deal of vivacity in my own way, but pray pass me, if you please, Mr. Churchill. I have nothing clever to say.

Mr. Elton:
Yes, pray pass me as well. As an old married man, I have nothing to say that can entertain Miss Woodhouse or any other young lady. Shall we walk, Mrs. Elton?

Mrs. Elton:
With all my heart.

(They stand and exit.)

Mr. Churchill:
Then Miss Woodhouse will hear my thoughts. I have so little confidence in my own judgment that whenever I marry, I hope she will choose a wife for me.

(turns to Emma)

Will you? Will you choose a wife for me? I am in no hurry; adopt her, educate her and make her life yourself.

Emma:

(glances at Harriet and then turns back to Mr. Churchill)

Very well, I undertake your commission. You shall have a charming wife.

Miss Fairfax:
I would like to see the view as well. Miss Smith, would you walk with me?

Harriet:
Ah…yes, I would be happy to.

(They stand and exit. Mr. Knightley enters.)

Mr. Knightley:
Emma, the carriages have arrived to take us back. Mr. Churchill, would you be so good as to inform the others?

Mr. Churchill:
Yes, of course.

(He stands and helps Emma stand and then exits.)

Mr. Knightley:
Emma, how could you be so unfeeling to Miss Bates? How could you be so insolent in your wit to a woman of her character, age and situation? I had not thought it possible of you.

Emma:
(tries to laugh it off)

How could I help saying what I did. It was not so very bad. I dare say she did not understand me.

Mr. Knightley:
I assure you she felt your full meaning. She has talked of nothing else since. I wish you could have heard her honoring your forbearance in being able to pay her such attentions, in the attention she receives from you and your father, when her society is so irksome.

Emma:
I know there is not a better creature in the world, but you must allow that what is good and what is ridiculous are most unfortunately blended in her.

Mr. Knightley:
They are blended, I acknowledge and were she a woman of fortune, I would not quarrel with you for any liberties of manner. But Emma, she is poor, and her situation should secure your compassion. You, whom she had known from an infant, from

whom her notice was an honor, to have you now, in a thoughtless and prideful moment, laugh at her. That was badly done indeed Emma.

(takes a deep breath)

This is not pleasant for you and it is very far from pleasant to me. But I must – I will – tell you truths while I can, satisfied with proving myself your friend by very faithful counsel.

(He turns and exits, leaving Emma alone on stage, shocked at the truth of her behavior.)

Scene 10

(The parlor at Hartsfield. Mr. Knightley, Harriet and Mr. Woodhouse are seated. Emma enters. Ad lib greetings.)

Mr. Woodhouse:
There you are my dear. It would appear that Highbury is being bereft of many of our friends. Mr. Weston called while you were out to say that Mr. Churchill received a letter this morning from his uncle with sad news; Mrs. Churchill has passed away. Mr. Weston said that his son left within the hour.

(Ad lib exclamations of surprise and sadness.)

Mr. Woodhouse:
And now, Mr. Knightley has come to say goodbye.

Emma:
(to Mr. Knightley)

You are leaving?

Mr. Knightley:
I am going to London, to spend a few days with John and Isabella, but I would not go away without seeing you and your father. Have you anything you wish me to convey to them?

Emma:
Nothing at all. But is not this a sudden trip?

Mr. Knightley:
Yes – no – I have been thinking of it for some time.

Mr. Woodhouse:
Well my dear, how were the Bateses and Miss Fairfax this morning?

(to Mr. Knightley and Harriet)

Emma went to call upon them first thing this morning. I daresay they were obliged to you for coming.

Emma:
I did not see Miss Fairfax, she was lying down with the headache, but Miss Bates received me and informed me that Miss Fairfax will be leaving them soon. She has accepted a position as a governess.

Harriet:
Poor Miss Fairfax.

Mr. Woodhouse:
Poor Miss Fairfax indeed and poor Miss Bates and Mrs. Bates. To not be able to provide for their own relative is a sad occurrence. I can only imagine what they must be going through. I know you will correspond with her, my dear Emma, to remind her of her friends.

(to Mr. Knightley and Harriet)

The kindness and charity you have given them must be a comfort.

Emma:
Charity, but not kindness; a virtue which some friends doubt I still have.

Mr. Knightley:
The truest friend does not doubt, but hopes.

(He smiles at her and she smiles shyly back.)

And now I must be off if I am to arrive before supper.

(bows)

Goodbye, Miss Smith. Mr. Woodhouse, I shall convey your letter to Isabella.

(takes Harriet's hand, looks at her eyes for a moment with a slight smile)

Goodbye, Emma.

Emma:
Goodbye Mr. Knightley.

Mr. Woodhouse:
If you will excuse me, Emma, Miss Smith, I am going to my study to compose a letter of condolence to Mr. Frank Churchill.

(he exits.)

Harriet:
Poor Mr. Churchill; to lose his aunt.

Emma:
I do sincerely pity Mr. Churchill, but no one who knows this situation, can fail but realize what this means to him.

Harriet:
What do you mean?

Emma:
Mrs. Weston told me that, while the elder Mr. Churchill was an easy, kind man who always was pleased with his nephew's choices, Mrs. Churchill was quite rigid in the control she had over her nephew and the decisions for his future.

(Harriet frowns in confusion)

Emma:
Don't you see, Harriet? Frank Churchill can marry whomever he

likes without fear of losing his inheritance.

Harriet:

(understanding now, but in control of her reactions.)

Oooohhhh….that is indeed a wonderful thing.

Scene 11

(The parlor at Hartfield several days later. Emma is seated reading. Mr. Woodhouse enters.)

Mr. Woodhouse:
Ah, there you are, my dear.

Emma:
Yes, I am expecting Harriet any moment now and while I wait I thought to read a book Mrs. Weston recommended to me when she was Miss Taylor.

Mr. Woodhouse:
I know she would be pleased. Speaking of Miss Taylor, a messenger just arrived from Randalls.

(he gives her a note.)

Miss Taylor sent a note to you.

Emma:
Oh?

(takes the note)

Thank you, Father. It is probably the recipe for that gruel you prefer.

Mr. Woodhouse:
Well, I am off, my dear, for my morning walk around the garden. Three turns is what Mr. Perry recommends. Have you seen my neck scarf?

Emma:

(stands and crosses to his chair, where the scarf is draped.)

Here it is, Father.

(crosses and wraps the scarf around his neck.)

Enjoy your walk.

(Mr. Woodhouse exits. Emma unfolds the note and begins to read.)

Emma:

My dear Miss Woodhouse, I have some news that is quite unsettling. In fact, it has caused Mr. Weston and me great agitation. As it has been ten days since Mrs. Churchill's decease, Mr. Weston and I have been momentarily expecting to hear news of Frank Churchill. Imagine our surprise when, instead of a letter, Mr. Churchill arrived at Randalls this morning.

(stops reading)

Frank Churchill has returned? I should tell Harriet when she arrives.

(continues reading)

Now I have news to tell you, my dear Miss Woodhouse, and I do not know quite how to break it to you.

(stops reading)

News?

(continues reading)

As I have mentioned him already, you might surmise the news relates to Mr. Frank Churchill, and you would be correct. His errand this morning was most extraordinary in nature. It is impossible to express our surprise. He came to speak to his father… to us… to announce his… engagement… to Jane Fairfax.

(stops reading)

Jane Fairfax?! You are not serious.

(continues reading)

You may well be amazed. Frank told us that they have been engaged since last October. This news hurt Mr. Weston and myself… for we had hoped that… another attachment… might have occurred.

(Emma crosses to the desk, sits down, takes pen and paper and begins writing.)

Emma:
My dear Mrs. Weston, you are correct in saying that I am amazed at your news. I will not pretend *not* to understand you when you speak of 'another attachment' and will give you all the relief in my power. Early in our acquaintance, I was very much disposed to be attached to Mr. Churchill. However, for these last three months, I have ceased to care for him as more than a friend. It was very wrong of Mr. Churchill to come among us and behave as if he were free to pursue the affections of any young woman. And how could Miss Fairfax bear such behavior? And to think that she was actually on the point of going into service as a governess. For him to allow her to suffer such a measure.

However, I am relieved for Jane; her days of insignificance are now over. And she will be able to care for her aunt and grandmother as well. Now Mrs. Bates will be able to have pork whenever she desires.

(Then she looks up in sudden realization.)

Harriet! Oh my poor friend. To be a second time the dupe of her misconceptions and a man's flattery. I am afraid this second disappointment will be more severe than the first. How shall I ever tell her?

Harriet:

(calling from offstage)

Miss Woodhouse.

Emma:
In here, Harriet.

(She hides the letter under her book as Harriet enters. She stands crosses to Harriet.)

Harriet:
Well, Miss Woodhouse, is not this the oddest news that ever was?

Emma:
What news do you mean?

Harriet:
About Jane Fairfax and Mr. Churchill. I met Mr. Weston just now as I was walking here and he told me himself. Imagine; Jane Fairfax and Mr. Frank Churchill have been privately engaged to one another this long while. Did you ever hear anything so strange? Had you any idea of his being in love with her?

Emma:
Upon my word, Harriet, can you seriously ask me whether I imagined him attached to another woman at the very time I was all but openly encouraging you to give way to your own feeling? You may be sure that – had I know – I would have cautioned you accordingly.

Harriet:
Me? Why should you caution me? You do not think I care about Mr. Churchill.

Emma:
You do not mean to deny that there was a time – and not very

distant either – when you gave me reason to understand that you cared about him?

Harriet:
Him? No, never! Dear Miss Woodhouse, how could you mistake me?

Emma:
Harriet? What do you mean? Mistake you?

Harriet:
I should not have though it possible that you misunderstood me. I know we agreed never to name him, but considering how infinitely superior he is to everybody else, I should not have thought it possible to suppose I meant anyone else. Frank Churchill indeed! And to think you have been so mistaken. I am sure, that but for believing you approved and encouraged me, I should have considered it a presumption to dare think of him. But if *you*, who have been always acquainted with him -

Emma:
Harriet! Let me understand...are you speaking of...Mr. Knightley.

Harriet:
To be sure I am. I thought you knew. When we talked about him, it was quite clear.

Emma:
Not quite clear. When you spoke of 'services rendered,' I was sure you meant the service Mr. Churchill rendered in protecting you from the gypsies.

Harriet:
Oh dear! It was not the gypsies I was thinking of. No! I was thinking of Mr. Knightley's coming and asking me to dance when Mr. Elton was so unkind as to not ask. That was the service which made me begin to feel how surpierior he was to every other.

Emma:

My goodness! This has been a most unfortunate – a most deplorable mistake! What is to be done?

Harriet:

I do not wonder that you should feel a great difference between us. You must think him five hundred million times above me. But if Mr. Knightley should really…if he does not mind the disparity, I hope, you will not set yourself against it.

Emma:

(pauses enough to calm down)

Have you any idea of Mr. Knightley's returning your affection?

Harriet:

(shyly)

Yes, I must say that I have. I never should have presumed to think of it but for you. You told me to observe him carefully and let his behavior be the rule and so I have. Now I seem to feel that I may deserve him.

Emma:

(struggles with herself)

Harriet, I will only venture to declare that Mr. Knightley is the last man in the world who would intentionally give any woman the idea of his feeling for her more than he really does.

Harriet:

(excited)

Oh, Miss Woodhouse, to hear you say that…to know that you approve…I feel so giddy…I had better go…I cannot compose myself and if your father were to see me in this state it would alarm him. Thank you, Miss Woodhouse…for everything!

(exits)

(Emma stares after Harriet for a moment and then turns, stunned, to sit down, as if her legs cannot support her.)

Emma:
How stupid I am! How blind I have been! Harriet and Mr. Knightley?

(stands and begins pacing)

All the blunders I have made trying to manage everyone else's heart that I do not know my own. If Mr. Knightley is to marry anyone

(stops and faces audience as she speaks in slow realization)

that someone… should surely… be me. I… love Mr. Knightley.

(slow smile in happiness of being in love then moves to sit down as a sad realization hits her.)

Too late… I'm too late… he loves Harriet… and this is all my own fault.

Scene 12

(The parlor at Hartfield. Mr. Woodhouse is sitting in his chair. Emma is tucking a blanket around him.)

Mr. Woodhouse:
What a long and melancholy day.

Emma:
Yes, it has been. The cold and gloomy rain causes one to forget that it is July. There, you are all covered.

Mr. Woodhouse:
(looking around his chair)

Where is my night cap? I know it was here somewhere. Mr. Perry assures me that if I do not protect my head, I will catch a cold or something worse.

Emma:

(finds his cap)

Here it is, Father.

(places it on his head)

There you go.

Mr. Woodhouse:

Thank you, my dear. You take such good care of me; what would I ever do without you?

Emma:

Do not worry, Father, for you will never have to face that possibility.

Mr. Woodhouse:

Yes, I know, my dear. You will always take care of me. You and Mr. Knightley. It has been difficult having him gone for so long. But when he returns from visiting John and Isabella, Mr. Knightley will resume visiting us and things will go on here at Hartfield as they always have.

Emma:

(pauses)

Yes…well, should something occur to prevent that…

Mr. Woodhouse:

Mr. Knightley has been stopping by daily for years. Whatever could occur to make him stop?

Emma:

I do not know, but…something…might happen.

Mr. Woodhouse:

(yawns)

My dear, you are letting this weather bring down your spirits. I know you miss visiting with Miss Taylor, but now that she has a wedding to plan, her days are filled.

(yawns again and begins to drift off to sleep.)

You should write your friend Miss Smith; she has not come to Hartfield lately.

(falls asleep)

(Emma leans over and kisses his forehead and then walks quietly over to sit down. She opens her diary and begins writing.)

Emma:

Dear Diary, I cannot tell my father that I do not wish to see Harriet; hearing her talk of Mr. Knightley would only irritate me. I wrote her today, advising her that all communication on that topic had better be avoided and to allow a few days to pass before we met again, in order that we might be able to act as if nothing had happened. She returned a note, approving of my suggestion.

I continue to try to not think about Mr. Knightley, but to no avail. I tried not to think about him when discussing the menu with Cook, only to realize I had included his favorite lamb stew. I tried not to think about him when I went to congratulate Jane Fairfax on her upcoming nuptials; only to have Miss Bates comment on the last wedding in Highbury. That brought to mind Mr. Knightley's question of who cried the most.

(Emma glances at her father, who is sleeping deeply. She sets her pen down and stands to kneel by the desk. She clasps her hand and prays.)

Emma:

Dear Lord, I have never wanted to be married and am content to remain thus. However, I cannot do it without my dear friend. If Mr. Knightley were to marry Harriet – or anyone – then life as we have known it would be over. If he cannot share a life with me, is it wrong to ask that he not share it with anyone? That we continue as we have gone on; him stopping by at any hour, dissipating every melancholy fancy…helping with Father…being a natural and easy member of the family. I would be content if he would just stay single, Lord. That would be enough for me to be perfectly satisfied. Well, almost satisfied…Amen.

Scene 13

(The garden at Hartfield. Emma enters, carrying a basket of flowers, when Mr. Knightley enters from the opposite side. They are obviously uncomfortable with each other.)

Emma:
Oh, Mr. Knightley. How do you do?

Mr. Knightley:
How do you do, Emma?

Emma:
When did you leave London?

Mr. Knightley:
Only this morning.

Emma:
You must have had a wet ride.

Mr. Knightley:
Yes I did.

Emma:
How are Isabella and John and the children?

Mr. Knightley:
They are well. I promised I would to convey their letters to you and your father when I first arrived.

(he hands her a small pack of letters wrapped with a ribbon.)

Emma:
Thank you.

(They pause for a moment without talking)

Emma:

(tries to be lighthearted)

You have some news to hear, now you are come back, that will rather surprise you.

Mr. Knightley:
Have I?

(looks at her intently, speaks quietly)

Of what nature?

Emma:
Of, the best nature in the world…a wedding.

Mr. Knightley:
If you mean Miss Fairfax and Frank Churchill, I have heard that already. Mr. Weston left me a list of parish business and included the news of the wedding. I read it before coming here.

(he looks at her)

Time, my dearest Emma, will heal the wound.

(He speaks to himself, in heated tones)

The feelings of the warmest friendship…misleading all who knew him…abominable scoundrel! Do not worry. He will soon be gone to Yorkshire. I am sorry for her; she deserves a better fate.

Emma:
You are very kind, but I must set you straight. I am not in want of your sympathies. For a brief time I…thought…I cared for Mr.

Churchill…but now I care nothing for him.

Mr. Knightley:
To find a wife that he loves and who loves him. While there are many things about him I dislike, in that respect he is the object of my envy.

Emma:
You…envy…him?

(pauses)

If there is anything you wish to tell me…as your friend..then I will hear it.

Mr. Knightley:
As a friend! Emma, I have no wish

(walks a few steps away and then stops and walks back)

Yes…why should I hesitate? I have gone too far already for concealment. Emma…tell me, then…have I no chance of ever succeeding?

(he pauses and when she doesn't speak, he continues)

My dearest Emma, for dearest you will always be, whatever the event of this hour's conversation, My dearest, most beloved Emma, tell me at once. Say, "No," if it is it to be said.

(she is still silent)

Mr. Knightley:
I cannot make speeches, Emma. If I loved you less, I might be able to talk about it more. But you know what I am. You hear nothing but truth from me. I have blamed you, lectured you and you have borne it as no other woman in England would have borne it. Bear with the truths I would tell you now, dearest Emma,. God knows

I have been a very indifferent lover. But you understand me, understand my feelings and I pray will return them. At present, I ask only to hear your voice.

(Emma turns and walks a few steps away and then turns back smiling. Mr. Knightley crosses to take her in his arms. Just before he kisses her, she pulls back.)

Emma:
Harriet!

Mr. Knightley:
Harriet? What are you talking about?

Emma:
She believes you are in love with her.

Mr. Knightley:
Why would she think that?

Emma:
Because you asked her to dance when Mr. Elton did not. She was willing to care for you from a distance, but because I thought she was referring to Mr. Churchill – who saved her from the gypsies – I encouraged her to believe that the feelings might be returned. After we learned that Mr. Churchill and Miss Fairfax were engaged, I learned that Harriet had actually meant you. She has been rejected two times; how can I be part of the reason she is rejected a third time? Are you sure you do not care for Harriet?

Mr. Knightley:
Ahhh…now I see. If I did care for Miss Smith, I might find a problem in Mr. Martin.

Emma:
Mr. Martin?

Mr. Knightley:
Yes. When I arrived home this morning, in addition to a note from

Mr. Weston, I also had a note from Mr. Martin. He informed me that his feelings for Miss Smith has never diminished—

Emma:
Poor Mr. Martin—

Mr. Knightley:
—and he asked for her hand once again.

Emma:
I hate to think of him being hurt—

Mr. Knightley:
—she she accepted him.

Emma:
What?

Mr. Knightley:
(taking her hands, smiling)

Apparently, Miss Smith discovered that she cared deeply for him and wanted to marry him above all others. Now that her heart will not be broken by me, is it alright if I am in love with you?

(Emma smiles at Mr. Knightley. He moves to take her in his arms. Just before he kisses her, Emma pulls out.)

Emma:
Father!

Mr. Knightley:
Your father?

Emma:
(upset)

I love you and I always will, but I cannot marry you! How can I leave him alone at Hartfield? He has spent the whole of my life terrified that something would separate us. He cannot bear it and I will not hurt him.

Mr. Knightley:
I care for your father too and would never hurt him. I think there is a solution.

Emma:
There is no solution.

Mr. Knightley:
(takes her hands)

Emma, my heart is where you are. What matters if that is at Hartfield or at Donwell Abbey? When we are married, we will live at Hartfield for as long as necessary.

Emma:
You would do that…for me, Mr. Knightley?

Mr. Knightley:
I would do anything for you, my dearest Emma. And if we are to be married, can you not call me George now?

Emma:
I have called you Mr. Knightley for so long I cannot conceive of calling you anything else.

Mr. Knightley:
Emma…

Emma:
Perhaps not now, but

(with a flirtatious air)

I will promise to call you by your Christian name. It will be when we are standing in a building where I will say, "I Emma Woodhouse, take thee *George* Knightley, to my wedded husband.

To have and to hold from this day forward. For better or for worse…

(Mr. Knightley stops this speech by kissing Emma.)

THE END

About the Playwright

Early training in music and theatre lead Paula K. Parker to a life-long love for the arts. This passion eventually brought her to Nashville, Tennessee where she, along with her husband, actor Mike Parker, helped establish three local community theatre companies. The couple continues to live in Middle Tennessee.

In addition to her stage plays, Ms. Parker is also an internationally acclaimed author, penning both fiction and non-fiction titles, including the two-volume ***Ancient Mysteries Retold*** series with NYT best-selling author, GP Taylor, ***Sisters of Lazarus: Beauty Unveiled***, ***Illuminations***, ***An Unlikely Evangelist*** and ***Shameless Self Promotion***.

Other Plays by Paula K. Parker

Jane Austen's Pride & Prejudice
Jane Austen's Sense & Sensibility
Bloodlines

To find out more about Paula K. Parker visit her online at www.paulakparker.com

To find out more about WordCrafts Theatrical Press visit www.wordcrafts.net

Made in the USA
Las Vegas, NV
10 April 2023

70445308R00074